D1333335

THE EARLY HORTICULTURISTS

THE
EARLY
HORTICULTURISTS

By

RONALD WEBBER

DAVID & CHARLES : NEWTON ABBOT

7153 4264 9

© RONALD WEBBER 1968

TO

MY WIFE

Printed in Great Britain for
David & Charles (Holdings) Limited
Newton Abbot Devon by
Clarke, Doble & Brendon Limited Plymouth

CONTENTS

LIST OF ILLUSTRATIONS

INTRODUCTION

HORTICULTURE, according to the *Oxford English Dictionary*, is the 'art of garden cultivation'. The word derives from the Latin *hortus*, a garden, so that a horticulturist is, therefore, a gardener.

In common usage, however, the two words do not have quite the same meaning, though the difference is not easy to define. A gardener (to quote the *O.E.D.* again) is 'a person who gardens, esp servant employed to tend a garden'. But what is a horticulturist?

Broadly, the horticulturist is someone engaged in any one of the many forms of horticulture. Apart from general gardening, these can include the commercial production of fruit, vegetables and flowers, plant breeding, landscape gardening, the raising of plants in nurseries, plant health, marketing, advising, teaching and so on.

Horticulture is regarded as an art but is connected with science at almost every point. It is also a department of agriculture, the horticulturist tending to deal with the more intensive forms of plant cultivation. It overlaps into botany.

Looking at it from another angle, it can be roughly split into two divisions, one associated with the home, the other with earning a living. The former is amateur gardening, the latter commercial horticulture.

The horticulturists whom I have chosen to write about were all in one way or other dependent on horticulture for their livelihood. The book starts with a brief account of horticulture through the ages and goes on to describe a handful of men (and one woman) who have contributed to the world of commercial horticulture in some way or other. Each represents a period or particular branch of horticulture. A few, like James Lee and John Tradescant, have already been the subject of whole books. Others, like Richard Harris and Sarah Sewell, are shadowy figures around whom I have built a story of the period.

9

But known or comparatively unknown—nurseryman, breeder, salesman, florist, market gardener, seedsman or what you will—together they represent a cross-section of the human material that goes to the making of the history of British horticulture.

I have included a bibliography, but this should be looked upon only as a starting point for research by anyone interested in a particular person or subject. There is plenty more to be found out.

To members of the families of Poupart, Rochford and Segar, may I say thank you for making available much material that is not to be found in books? For my story of Thomas Smith, my thanks are due to his son Bertram, who lent me an unpublished manuscript in which Thomas Smith describes his early life. For the story of A. W. Smith, my thanks go to the *Middlesex Chronicle*, which produced a bound volume of newspaper cuttings about him.

Acknowledgement is gratefully made to the staffs of the many libraries and societies who have helped me in the search for material, particularly to those of the British Museum, Greater London Council, Westminster Local History Library, Guildhall and Camden.

My thanks, too, to my wife, who undertook the onerous task of converting the original manuscript into a readable typescript, and to John Turpin who so conscientiously read the typescript.

CHAPTER ONE

COMMERCIAL HORTICULTURE
UNTIL 1900

U P to the time of the Norman Conquest, only a limited range of fruits and vegetables was used as food by the inhabitants of Britain. Plants growing wild had no doubt been gathered and eaten from the earliest days, and as far back as the Neolithic Age (2500 BC), it is thought that women may have started to cultivate a few plants, scratching the soil with primitive tools to make room for a few good specimens of fruit and vegetables which they had sampled in their wild state and found edible. By the Late Bronze Age (1000 BC), when the first plough replaced the hoe in agriculture, it was possible to cultivate on a larger scale, but it is not until the La Tene culture of the Early Iron Age (250 BC) that vegetables are definitely known to have been cultivated.

Outside Britain, early civilizations had grown a wide range of crops. Cabbage, asparagus, peas, beans, seakale and onions were known to the Greeks. The Romans cultivated peas, beans, turnips, carrots, parsnips, beet, radish, sorrel, asparagus, onions, garlic, cucumbers, chicory, lettuce, parsley, mustard, mushrooms, as well as many herbs. In fruits, they had the apple, peach, grape, plum, cherry, mulberry, almond, medlar, pear and quince.

Before the Romans came, the vegetables grown in Britain were probably mainly developments from the cabbage, asparagus and seakale, all of which grew wild. Other wild plants, such as chicory and celery, were no doubt left until someone discovered that they could be made much more edible by blanching the stems. Leeks grew wild in certain places by the sea and a few chives could possibly have been found along the streams of Cornwall and Northumberland. Wild fruits such as apples, plums, cherries, gooseberries and currants were no doubt picked and eaten. The Romans, however, are generally given the credit for introducing the orchard and herb garden and for considerably extending the range of vegetables. But though they grew a wide range in their own country, it does not necessarily follow that all these were introduced to Britain. And with orchards, the idea of growing fruit trees together in a group near the farmhouse, though possibly a Roman innovation, does not mean that apples were not grown before that time. Tacitus, writing in the first century, claimed that the climate of Britain was suitable for the cultivation of all vegetables and fruits except the olive and vine.

When the Romans left, many of the plants they had introduced may have disappeared and it is not until the coming of the Saxons in the fifth century that it is possible to re-establish some idea of what was being grown. Apples were then the chief fruit crop, being grown mainly for the making of cider. Also to be found were pears, plums, chestnuts, hazel nuts and perhaps medlars, peaches and mulberries. Among vegetables, leeks had become popular—so much so that the kitchen garden was often called the leek garden and the gardener the 'leekward'. But the garden could also have contained cabbages, peas, turnips, lettuce, parsley, parsnips, onions, mint, garlic, and perhaps globe artichokes and beet.

The next 500 years was a period of very slow development. By 1300, apples are beginning to be given names such as pearmain and costard; pearmain seems to have been a general name but the costard was a particularly large apple and possibly a definite variety. It is from this word 'costard' that costermonger —seller of costards—derives. In pears, the name Warden appears—a variety cultivated by the Cistercian monks of Warden Abbey in Bedfordshire. Wild strawberries and raspberries were beginning to be transplanted into gardens and better types and varieties cultivated. Orchards were widespread, but fruit was also brought in from abroad. A garden was an essential part of all monastic institutions and vegetables were extensively grown in them. In counties such as Worcestershire, every manor and most farms possessed gardens and orchards, many of them very large.

London had probably the first true market gardeners, for it was easily the largest and most important city of the Middle

Ages and not every citizen had a garden or perhaps wanted to grow his own food. For many years before 1345 the gardeners of the earls, barons, bishops and others sold surplus produce near the gate of St Paul's churchyard, but by that year the market had grown to such an extent that it hindered the traffic 'both on foot and on horseback'. Also, the 'scurrility, clamour and nuisance' of the gardeners brought complaints from the local inhabitants and the authorities had to step in and move the market to a new site.

Some of the men who sold outside St Paul's no doubt called themselves gardeners, other preferred to be known as fruiterers. The Worshipful Company of Fruiterers was not granted its charter until 1605, but its records go back to 1292 when 'Gerin the Fruter' was selling fruit. The Gardeners' Company, which also received its charter in 1605, has scrapbooks dating from 1345. But precisely what, and how much these gardeners sold is difficult to say, as there is little information about the supply of fruit and vegetables in British towns at this time.

Famine was usual in bad years and there does not appear to have been any method of storing the surplus of a good year against the advent of a bad one. There is a theory that vegetables were widely grown and popular in the thirteenth and fourteenth centuries, but later fell into disuse. Harrison, in his *Description of England* written in 1577, says:

> Such herbes, fruits, & roots also, as grow yeerelie out of the ground, of seed, haue been verie plentifull in this land in the time of the first Edward, and after his daies: but in processe of time they grew also to be neglected, so that from Henrie the fourth till the latter end of Henrie the seuenth, & beginning of Henrie the eight, there was little or no vse of them in England, but they remained either vnknowne, or supposed as food more meet for hogs & sauage beasts to feed vpon, than mankind.

Printing did not start till 1497, so the surviving fifteenth-century English works on gardening are in manuscript. One, written about 1440 by 'Mayster Ion Gardener', gives a list of seventy-eight plants suitable for cultivation. Most are herbs to be used in the kitchen or for medicinal purposes. Of the more general garden vegetables, 'Mayster Ion' mentions radish, spinach, cabbage, lettuce, onions, garlic and leeks. Another manuscript of about the same date and quoted by Alicia Amherst in *A History of Gardening* refers to 'parsenepys', 'turnepez', 'karettes' and 'betes'. G. W. Johnson in *A History of English Gardening*, put the decline down to 'a still lingering taste for hunting, chivalry and war; by crusades to the Holy Land, and as wild expeditions to the Continent; and above all by the civil horrors induced by the contest between the houses of York and Lancaster'.

Herbs were, of course, grown extensively, and included not only the ordinary kitchen herbs of today—rosemary, sage, fennel, parsley, borage, marjoram and so on—but cultivated varieties of many of the herbs we now tend to look upon as weeds. An important use of these herbs was to provide flavouring for meat which could be 'high' during warm days in summer and rather insipid in winter, because it had to be salted in order to keep it. Of Griselda in Chaucer's *Clerk's Tale* it is written:

> And whan she homward came, she wolde bring
> Wortes and other herbes times oft,
> The which she shred and sethe for hire living.

Saffron was used in large quantities for cooking and was chiefly grown in the eastern counties. Walsingham, in Norfolk, was particularly famous for its saffron and the plant also gave its name to the town of Saffron Walden in Essex.

By the time of Henry VIII, a much wider range of fruit and vegetables, both homegrown and from the Continent, had become available. Melons, 'pompions' (pumpkins) and gourds of all kinds began to appear and there were plenty of the traditional leeks, onions and garlic. Globe artichokes are now mentioned frequently—their chief use seems to have been for boiling in beef broth. A cauliflower is pictured in John Gerard's *Herball* but it does not seem to have been common. The orchards now contained gooseberries, cherries, apricots, peaches, nectarines, raspberries, bullaces, plums, damsons and red currants. Barberries and whortleberries were also being cultivated.

The practice of growing vegetables, not only in the gardens of wealthy landowners but also in the small plots of the cottages, developed rapidly towards the end of the sixteenth century. Harrison, in his *Description of England*, says :

> Whereas in my time their vse is not onlie resumed among the poore commons,—I meane of melons, pompions, gourds, cucumbers, radishes, skirets, parsneps, carrets, cabbages, naeuewes (rape), turneps, and all kinds of salad herbes,—but also fed vpon as deintie dishes at the tables of delicate merchants, gentlemen, and the nobilitie, who make for their prouision yearelie for new feeds out of strange countries, from whence they haue them aboundantlie.

Imports of fruit and vegetables from the Continent also began to increase. Onions from Flanders were extremely popular, and Holland supplied most of the salad vegetables. But there seems to have been no shortage of home-grown fruits if a document by John Coke, *A Debate between the Heralds of England and France*, published in 1549, is to be believed.

> Item, we have almaner of graynes and fruites, and more plenty than you; for, thanked be God! England is a fruitful and plenteous region, so that we have sum fruites whereof you have fewe, as wardeines, quynces, peches, medlers, chestnottes, and other delycious fruytes serving for all seasons of the yere, and so plenty of peres and aples, that in the weste partes of England and Sussex they make pirry and sydre, and in such habundaunce that they convaye parte over the sea, where by the Monseurs of France it is coveted for theyr beverages and drynkes.

This may have been propaganda but it does appear that England lacked little. Yet according to the *The Fruiterer's Secrets* published anonymously in 1604, most of the fruit trees were brought in from France and the Low Countries as late as the reign of Henry VIII. They were introduced, according to this account, by Richard Harris, the King's fruiterer, about 1533. The first pippin apples, however, are said to have been introduced by Leonard Mascall from the Continent twenty years earlier and grown in an orchard in Sussex.

In the sixteenth century, Kent was the leading county growing fruit for market. W. Lambard in his *A Perambulation of Kent,* 1596, says :

> In fertile and fruitful woodes and trees this county is most floryshing also whether you respecte the maste of oke, beeche,

and chesten for cattail : or the fruit of aples, peares, cherries, and ploumes for men . . . as for orchards of aples, and gardeins of cherries and those of the most exquisite and delicious kindes that can be, no part of the Realme (that I know) hath them, either in such quantitie and number, or with such arte and industrie set and planted.

Kent's leading position was mainly due to its proximity to London, for the poor state of the roads of that time precluded sending such perishable produce over long distances. Kent also had a fertile soil and a favourable climate. Another reason was that the open fields system of strip cultivation, common in other parts of the country in the sixteenth century, was never so dominant in Kent. Once the monasteries had been broken up, Kent did not develop into a county of large landowners. Instead, farmers frequently owned the land they farmed, and as this was often one complete unit, they were encouraged to plant up orchards.

The growing of apples and pears was also well advanced in Herefordshire, Gloucestershire and Worcestershire, though in these parts the fruit was mainly grown for cider or perry.

Apples were always the most important fruit in Britain. Besides being extensively used for eating, cooking and making cider, they were also in favour at one time as a cosmetic. Gerard, in his *Herball*, says that the cosmetic was employed to soften the skin and take away freckles. To the pulp of apples was added rose water and swine's grease, the resulting concoction being sold under the name of 'pomatum'. The cooking apple 'Pomewater' was said to be the best variety to use.

John Parkinson, in his *Paradisi in Sole Paradisus Terrestris* published in 1629, says of apples :

The best sorts . . . serve at the last course for the table, in most mens houses of account; where if there grow any rare or excellent fruit, it is then set forth to be seene and tasted. Divers other sorts serve to bake, either for the Masters Table or the meynes sustenance, either in pyes or pans, or else stewed in dishes with Rosewater and Sugar and Cineman or Ginger cast upon. Some kinds are fittest to roast in the winter time, to warme a cup of wine, ale or beere, or to be eaten alone, for the nature of some fruit is never so good or worth the eating, as when they

Ploughing and sowing in the sixteenth century.

John Sutton, a pioneer seedsman.

Nonpareil apple.

London market gardens of the sixteenth century.

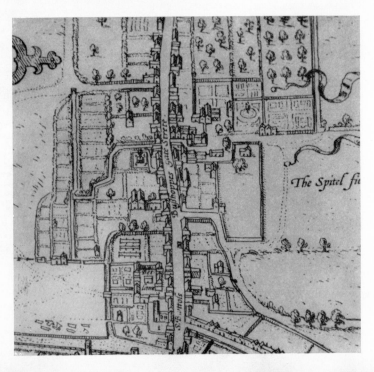

are roasted. Some sorts are fitted to scald for codlins and are taken to coole the stomache, as well as to please the taste, having Rosewater and Sugar put to them. Some sorts are best to make Cider of as in the West Countrey of England great quantities, yea many Hogsheads and Tunnes full are made, especially to be carried to the Sea in long voyages : and it is found by experience to be of excellent use to mix with water for beverage. It is usually seen that those fruits that are neither fit to eate raw, roasted nor baked, are fittest for cider and make the best. The juice of Apples, likewise as of pippins and pearmains, is of very good use in Melancholic diseases, helping to produce mirth and to expel heaviness. The distilled water of the same apples is of like effect.

At the beginning of the reign of Queen Elizabeth, British horticulture received a fillip from an influx of Protestant refugees from the Continent, a number of whom brought with them that skill in intensive market gardening for which the Dutch, Walloons and French had been famous for many years. The coast towns of Kent, Essex and Suffolk received the main stream of these refugees.

In 1561, a considerable body landed near Deal and from there moved on to the then decayed town of Sandwich. They were mostly from West Flanders, a one-time province of France. Other landings of Flemings took place at Harwich, Yarmouth, Dover and other towns on the south-east coast.

Sandwich had at one time been a town of considerable import-ance and one of the Cinque Ports. But in the second half of the sixteenth century it had become almost deserted and the Flemish refugees practically took it over; by 1573 they constituted about half the population.

Market gardening was one of the several branches of industry they introduced. Finding suitable soil around Sandwich, they began to develop vegetable growing and very soon, according to Samuel Smiles writing nearly 300 years later in *The Huguenots* :

the cabbage, carrots and celery produced by the foreigners met with so ready a sale and were so much in demand in London itself, that a body of gardeners shortly afterwards removed from Sandwich and settled at Wandsworth, Battersea and Bermondsey where many of the rich garden-grounds first planted

B

by the Flemings, still continue to be the most productive in the neighbourhood of the metropolis.

It is unlikely that Sandwich itself afforded sufficient scope for market gardening on a large scale. Its population and those of the neighbouring towns would not have been large enough to warrant growing crops commercially merely to meet local demands, particularly as most of the houses would have had some kind of garden of their own in which to grow fruit and vegetables. And, as a port, Sandwich was already too decayed to attract ships to come in and take the food away. What possibly happened was that the London merchants who came to Sandwich to buy the cloth of the weavers appreciated the high quality of the vegetables which were being grown and took samples back to eat and to show their friends. Cabbages, celery and carrots could all stand up to the long journey to London either by road or water. The Sandwich market gardeners also made a name as seedsmen.

Another town to which the Flemings went from Sandwich was Norwich and here too they introduced the art of intensive market gardening. Samuel Smiles says 'Culinary stuffs became more plentiful in Norwich than in any other town or city in England'. But Norwich was already a large and important town and herbs, leeks, fruit and other vegetables had been sold in the town's market from very early times.

How the foreigners were received by the market gardeners in London is not known, though a petition in 1615 from the Gardeners' Company to the Lord Mayor states that they (the Gardeners)

> desire not . . . to restrain any forreyners to bringe into the cittie anie such commodities as they sell, for the fundamental lawes of this land give to all men whatsoever, libertie soe to doe in regard that they bring victuall wholesome and according to the lawes.

Possibly the rapid increase of the population was providing enough work for all. The chief problem (in London at least) was finding somewhere suitable to sell the produce. Much of it was hawked from house to house, but street markets were still the favourite places for anyone with a large quantity to sell and the market gardeners were always trying to find still better ones.

The Stocks Market, 'les Stokkes', on the site of the present Mansion House, had been in use since early in the fourteenth century and was rebuilt close by the site of St Mary Woolchurch after the Great Fire chiefly for the sale of fruits and vegetables, though it had a limited capacity.

From very early days, too, there had been a market of sorts near the southern end of London Bridge. It was opposite Billingsgate Market on the other bank of the river and, until the Romans came, there was no bridge to link the two places. This market is mentioned in 1276, when it made such a nuisance of itself by spreading across the bridge that trading on it was made illegal.

In the seventeenth century, when the Covent Garden area was laid out by Inigo Jones as a residential area for the gentry, the market gardeners began to creep in and display their goods for sale alongside the garden wall of Bedford House, which formed the south boundary of the new 'piazza'. Trade developed quickly and a charter authorising the Earl of Bedford to hold an official market there was obtained in 1670.

Spitalfields, on the opposite side of London, received its charter eleven years later and this allowed one John Balch to hold two markets a week 'in or next a certain place called the Spittle Square'. Most of its produce came from market gardeners in the neighbourhood, though a few lived as far away as Blackheath and Lewisham. One well-known market gardener who had a stand there was John Abercombie, a writer of popular gardening books.

By the end of the eighteenth century, the riverside from the Three Crane Stairs directly south of the Guildhall to Queenhithe was given over almost entirely to the wholesale fruit trade. Billingsgate was the most important harbour for landing vegetables for the City markets, and large quantities of cherries and other fruit from Kent also arrived there. Dealers swarmed in the lanes around this area and near the river there was an open market with a roof supported by poles where fruit was often auctioned before going to Covent Garden and other markets.

From such London ports as these, regular sailings were made up the Thames and a big trade was done in manure and street sweepings for use on the market gardens. These materials, as well as others such as bones and ashes, could be delivered to any place on the Thames capable of being reached in one tide—which is one good reason why market gardeners kept close to the river in those early days. Boats also went up the River Lea, taking dung to the Enfield area.

As the population of Britain grew, so the cultivation of produce for human consumption increased with it. By the end of the seventeenth century, fruit and vegetable growing was recognised as an important industry, and a special branch of it, the 'nursery' trade, was busy raising or selecting seedlings of choice plants or trees, or growing-on chance seedlings which showed promise. Many new species and varieties coming in from foreign countries were being propagated and sold by the nurserymen. When, a little later, the scientific breeding of plants began, a much wider range of varieties became available.

During the eighteenth century, this profession of nurseryman developed considerably and some began to set themselves up as experts in laying out and planting up orchards and gardens. Nurserymen such as Stephen Switzer, Thomas Fairchild and Thomas Hitt, all of whom wrote practical books on fruit growing, were garden designers as well. Nurseries selling plants and trees became numerous.

Still more new plants were now coming in from abroad. The modern large red strawberry, for example, was evolved from varieties introduced from Carolina and from China by way of Holland early in the eighteenth century. Varieties of apples were constantly increasing, many new sorts of gooseberries were grown—green, yellow, white, red, black and striped—and a number of new varieties of cherry were introduced.

Among vegetables, carrots became more popular and potatoes flourished in Essex, Yorkshire, Lancashire and the North, though it was not until the end of the century that they began to be grown on a large scale in Norfolk, Kent and the west of England. Saffron was still grown in Essex and woad in Northamptonshire. Madder continued to be produced on a small scale in Surrey and Kent, and the Vale of Pickering made quite a name for itself with tobacco cultivation. Salsify and celery also came into prominence.

An eighteenth-century visitor to England who mentions market gardening is Pehr Kalm, a Swede who was sent to North America in 1748 to bring back new plants and visited England on his way. He says that, near London, market gardens appeared in several places 'together with very large fields which the market gardeners rented and had sown with everything required in kitchens'. Most of the gardens, he reported, were covered with glass frames with Russian matting on top and this covered with straw. Bell glasses were also being used for protection. Many of the gardens had high thick earth walls, generally with a ditch on the outside to stop cattle from getting in. And many walls had glass embedded on top to keep out thieves.

John Middleton, in his *General View of the Agriculture of Middlesex*, 1790, says that from Kensington through Hammersmith, Chiswick, Brentford, Isleworth and Twickenham, the land on both sides of the road was mostly fruit for the supply of London. The ground, he says, 'was well stocked with apples, pears, cherries, plums and walnuts; among them were grown raspberries, currants, strawberries and all such herbs and shrubs as will sustain the drips of trees'.

But it was not until the middle of the nineteenth century that market gardening and fruit growing became a major industry. The first thirty years of the century was a period of heavy taxes, restricted liberty and penal laws. But after the battle of Waterloo things began to improve. In 1846 the Corn Laws were repealed and about the same time came the abolition of window tax and taxes on timber and bricks, all of which helped the horticultural industry to develop. More advanced types of machines and implements began to appear, and there was a much more scientific approach to manuring and dressing the soil. Farmers were also becoming interested in market garden crops suitable for large-scale mechanical cultivation. Vegetables and fruit were improved by selective breeding and culture, though few new plants other than the tomato were introduced for commercial use. Tomatoes had been known as far back as 1544, when they had come into Europe by way of Mexico. But these early tomatoes were ribbed, rather ugly fruit, which were grown more as a curiosity and regarded in Britain as unfit for eating, though known to be enjoyed by Spaniards and other foreigners. In the nineteenth century, a mutation occurred which brought the smooth round two-chambered tomato and on this mutant an industry began to build up.

Watercress was promoted from its wild state (in which form it had been sold for many years) to cultivated beds at the beginning of the nineteenth century. The first of these was at Springhead, near Northfleet in Kent.

In 1801, the population of Greater London had been just over one million. By 1820 it had reached one and a half million and by 1900 had leapt to over six million. More room was needed for houses and market gardeners who possessed land suitable for building had to move further out. Much the same process was taking place in other parts of the country.

It was not only the spread of population that pushed the market gardeners out of the big towns. The coming of the steam railway in mid-century also influenced the location of market gardens in two ways. First, the close network of railway lines which rapidly built up, especially round London, ran through many a market garden. It is true that an Act of Parliament had to be passed every time a new railway was laid, but in 1846 alone 246 separate Acts were passed. The owners of the land over which the lines passed usually received adequate compensation and when the owner also happened to be the market gardener himself (for much of the land was rented), he was often able to start afresh with a larger piece of land in another area.

The second effect of the coming of the railways was that the very railway which took away a market gardener's land often enabled him to set up in a part of the country where the soil was favourable but which had previously been too far from a town to be suitable for market garden work. In Bedfordshire, for example, market gardening had been established as early as the seventeenth century but did not develop to any extent until the railway came and distant markets became easily accessible.

In Cornwall, at the beginning of the nineteenth century, many thousands of bushels of new potatoes were being sent every season by sea from west Cornwall to Plymouth and Portsmouth. The cauliflower trade started around 1836 and that of straw-berries during the 1860s. In the close-by Isles of Scilly, a cut flower business started with the semi-wild narcissus 'Soleil d'Or', and by 1879 a flourishing commercial trade had been established with the London markets. Early potatoes were also grown.

Market gardening in Worcestershire is thought to have owed its early start to the monks attached to the great abbey of Evesham. By 1768, when Arthur Young, Secretary to the Board of Agriculture, visited Evesham, the area of market garden land there was between 300 and 400 acres and the produce was being sold as far afield as Birmingham, Worcester, Tewkesbury, Gloucester, Warwick, Bath and Bristol. Evesham asparagus had already become famous.

Lancashire, the Channel Islands, Yorkshire, Derbyshire, Lincolnshire, Norfolk, Suffolk and many other places started growing vegetables, fruit and flowers on a large scale because the advent of the railway and motor transport made marketing so much easier. At the same time, market gardens were being set up outside all large towns to cater for the local trade.

The importation of overseas produce was also helped by this improvement in communications. In the early part of the nineteenth century pineapples, melons, currants, oranges and lemons were being brought from as far off as the West Indies by small fast merchant schooners. Refrigeration had not arrived, so speed was essential if the cargo was to arrive in good condition. About, 1880, refrigeration was introduced into ships and trains and this allowed a much wider range of produce to come in at prices within the reach of the ordinary person. By 1898, refrigerated ships were bringing fruit from as far away as Australia.

Another important development of the nineteenth century was the glasshouse industry. The first real glasshouse in Britain was probably one erected at the Apothecaries' Garden at Chelsea in 1684. It consisted of a room with glass windows and was heated by hot embers placed in a hole in the floor. By the early eighteenth century glass roofs had been introduced, but not until 1790 was steam used for heating. In 1837, Joseph Paxton, head gardener to the Duke of Devonshire, built the largest glasshouse in the world, 277 ft by 123 ft, and followed this up in 1851 by what eventually became the Crystal Palace in London.

About 1860, glasshouses were put up in the Worthing area of

JENKINS'
NURSERY,
REGENT'S PARK,

To Noblemen, Gentlemen, Nursery-men, Market Gardeners, & others.

A CATALOGUE
Of the Valuable
NURSERY STOCK
To be Sold by Auction,
WITHOUT RESERVE,
BY

PROTHEROE & MORRIS,

On the Premises,
INNER CIRCLE, REGENT'S PARK,
On Monday, October 20, 1834,
AND FOLLOWING DAYS,
AT ELEVEN O'CLOCK,
By Order of the Executors :

Comprising Standard and Dwarf Apples, Pears, Plums, Cherries, Walnuts, Standard & Dwarf Trained Peaches, Nectarines, Apricots, Pears, Plums, Cherries, Elm, Ash, Limes, Birch, Beech, Oak, Chesnut, Poplars, Thorns, Sycamore, Laburnums ; Portugal Laurels, Laurels, Privets; Rhododendrons, Azalea, Andromeda, Lilac, Acacia, Syringa, &c. &c. &c.

May be Viewed One Week previous to Sale, Catalogues 1s. each, (returnable to Purchasers,) may be had of Mr. BUNNY Conservatory, Covent Garden,—Messrs. Flanagan and Nutting, Seedsmen, Mansion House Street.—Messrs. Gray & Son, Seedsmen, Kensington,—Messrs. Wilmot, Lewisham,—Messrs. Nash and Co, Strand,—Messrs Thatcher, Seedsmen, Islington,—on the Premises, and of the Auctioneers, Highbury Nursery, and High Street Kingsland.

MULLIN, Printer, 3, Circus Street, New Road.

A nursery sale announcement of 1834.

Sussex and by 1874 there was nearly an acre covered by glass in that area. By 1880, one man alone at Worthing had a nursery covering sixteen acres and containing 106 glasshouses. Seventy years later, the area had spread all along the Sussex coast and in west Sussex alone there were 270 acres of glass.

Development of glasshouses in north London took place about the same time. In 1862, glasshouses with large squares of glass instead of the small ones previously used appeared and these houses were soon to be found in many parts of Tottenham, Enfield and Finchley. In the 1880s, when building developments in north London compelled growers to seek more rural sites, many moved out into the Lea Valley around Cheshunt, Hoddesdon and Waltham Cross, an area which offered ample supplies of water and suitable soil for glasshouse crops. It was also fairly close to London, with its ever increasing demand for choice produce. At first, traditional crops such as flowers, ferns, cucumbers, melons and grapes were produced, but soon newer and larger houses were going up for the tomato, which was fast catching on. By the turn of the century, about 300 acres of glass had been constructed.

The glasshouse industry in Kent started about 1870, about the same time that growers in the Blackpool area were laying the foundations of what was to become an extensive industry. The Hampton district of Middlesex went over to glass about 1884 and in almost every county of England glasshouse nurseries were to be found either catering for the needs of local populations or using the new railways to take the produce to far-off markets.

The smaller grower who could not afford the large glasshouses turned instead to 'French gardening', an intensive form of culture using cloches, frame lights and hot beds, which the market gardeners around Paris had been successfully practising for several centuries.

In Scotland, apples and pears, cherries, gooseberries and currants were being cultivated at the end of the fourteenth century and some vegetables were also being grown. By the end of the seventeenth century, much wider ranges of both vegetables and fruit were available and Edinburgh, in particular, enjoyed a high reputation for its produce. In the early part of the eighteenth century most of Edinburgh's vegetables were brought into the city from the Musselburgh area, but by 1771 there were thirty-two market gardens in the Edinburgh district and double that number by 1812. From 1870 onwards, strawberries and raspberries became increasingly popular crops with Scottish growers but as transport improved both at home and abroad, locally-grown apples became difficult to dispose of against the competition of the better quality imported fruit and acreages were soon drastically reduced. Glasshouses (for tomatoes) were first built in the Clyde Valley about 1895.

The marketing side of commercial horticulture in Britain began to take on a more important aspect towards the end of the nineteenth century and, in the wholesale markets, businesses were set up to handle home-grown and imported produce on commission. Until then, most growers had brought their own produce to the market and sold it themselves. The growing of seeds became a big business—supplying both the commercial grower and the general public. The florist shop also made its appearance about this time and, when the twentieth century opened, commercial horticulture had become firmly established in all its branches.

CHAPTER TWO

RICHARD HARRIS OF TEYNHAM

WITH the Tudors established on the throne of England and life becoming rather more affluent, people began to show interest in a wider range of fruit for the table. Apples and pears were already being grown extensively, mainly in the West Country, for the making of cider and perry, but little attention had been given to dessert fruit. That high-quality fruit of this type was available became increasingly known as trade with the more horticulturally advanced countries such as Holland and France expanded. Specimen trees and grafts of good dessert varieties had already been obtained and were being grown in a few British private gardens. But with more and more people becoming interested in eating good dessert fruit, the stage was set for fruit-growing on a commercial scale.

Most of our popular cultivated fruits can be found growing in a wild form in Britain and modern varieties have either developed from these or have been introduced from abroad. The earliest kinds of apples were wildings, mainly of the crab apple, and were used for cider. If a particular variety of cider apple was sweet enough, it was no doubt eaten, especially by children who, as today, know which varieties of cider apple are good to eat, But no one bothered at first about cultivating special varieties for eating.

The making of cider goes back a very long way; even in prehistoric times it is believed that some method of fermenting the juice of the wild crab apple was known and practised. The wassailing of apple trees to make them fruitful, a ritual carried out in the West Country until quite recent times, was of pagan origin. In the Welsh, Cornish and Irish languages the apple is 'avall' or 'aball', and the Hoedue who dwelt in Somerset ranked it so high that their town, which stood on the site of present-day Glastonbury was known as Avallonia or 'apple orchard'. The making of perry from pears is also a very old practice and there are references to it dating back to the third century.

As medieval times drew to a close, greater intercourse with the Continent began to influence fruit growing. The Normans no doubt brought new varieties of fruit with them once they settled down after the 1066 invasion, for Normandy was then well ahead of Britain in fruit culture.

Both cider apples and perry pears were important crops in the West Country from the Norman Conquest onwards. In 1310, for example, one Joan, widow of John Muchegros of Worcester, was accused of 'unlawfully cutting down 100 pear trees and 100 apple trees each worth 2s'. The arms of the city of Worcester bear 'three pears sable', which were added at the desire of Queen Elizabeth when she visited Worcester in 1575 and she would hardly have made the suggestion had pear-growing not been an important industry. (Though she may have been somewhat influenced by the action of the enthusiastic citizens of Worcester in setting up a pear tree in full fruit in the centre of the town so that she could not fail to see it.)

Whether the pears were worth eating is another matter. A sixteenth-century manuscript quoted by R. C. Gaut in *A History of Worcestershire Agriculture* warns about over-indulgence :

> Peres causeth ye colyck passion in ye bowlles, wyld peres stoppeth and noyeth ye stomake, but ye grete tame peres byn better usid in meates than the lyttle, and the juice of both usid before dyner stopeth ye bely, and usid after dyner layeth ye bely.

Over on the east side of England, fruit growing was subject to influences from the Continent from an early date. In 1204, the manor of Runham in Norfolk was held by Robert de Evermere who, on the feast of St Michael, had to pay the Exchequer 200 pearmains and four hogsheads of wine made from pearmains. (Pearmain at that period probably stood for a particularly large apple of any sort, though it was to develop as a named variety later on.) The garden of a Norwich monastery in 1340 sold apples and pears which brought in 13s 4½d.

Plums and cherries were also eaten, though, until the sixteenth century, most of the really edible ones would have been imported.

By the time of Henry VIII, fruit was beginning to be enjoyed both as a dessert and for cooking, the best having still to be brought in from the Continent and therefore much too expensive for the ordinary person. The aristocracy began to bring in trees for planting in their private gardens but it was Henry VIII, so far as we know, who, at the age of twenty-four, first encouraged the growing of fruit on a commercial scale. This was at Teynham, near Sittingbourne, in Kent in 1533.

The first report of the work comes from W. Lambard in *A Perambulation of Kent*, first published in 1576. In describing the area, Lambard says that Teynham and thirty parishes round about were the 'Cherrie gardein and apple orcharde of Kent'. He continues:

> where our honest patriote Richard Harrys (Fruiterer to King Henrie the 8) planted by his great coste and rare industrie, the sweete cherry, the temperate Pipyn, and the golden renate. For this man, seeing that this Realme (which wanted neither the favour of the sunne, nor the fat of the soile, meete for the making of good apples) was neverthelesse served chiefly with that fruit from forreign Regions abroad . . . and those planted which our ancestores had brought hither out of Normandie had lost their native verdour whether you did eate their substance or drink their juice for cider, . . . he, (I say) about the yeere of our Lord Christ 1533 obtained 105 acres of good ground in Tenham, then called Brennet, which he divided into ten parcels . . . and with great care, good choice, and no small labour and cost, brought plantes from beyonde the seas, and furnished this ground with them, so beautifully as they not onely stand in most right lines but seem to be of one sorte, shape and fashion, as if they had been drawen thorow one mould, or wrought by one and the same patterne.

Lambard here calls the area of ground at Teynham that Harrys (or Harris) planted, the 'Brennet'. This name no longer exists but according to E. Selby's *Teynham Manor and Hundred*, a pencilled note on the manor rolls of Teynham states that Oziers Farm is the actual site of the 'Brennet'. Local tradition has it that Harris first planted a few cherries in the Brennet and then went on to plant the New Garden on a much bigger scale.

This planting of so large an acreage for fruit must have caused quite a sensation in the horticultural world of the mid-sixteenth

century. The first horticultural writer to mention it is the unknown author of *The Husbandman's Fruitfull Orchard* in 1608,
who says :

> One Richard Harris, of London, borne in Ireland, fruiterer to
> King Henry the eight, fetched out of Fraunce great store of
> graftes, especially pippins : before which time there was no
> right pippins in England. He fetched also, out of the Lowe
> Countries, cherrie grafts and peare grafts of divers sorts : Then
> tooke a peece of ground belonging to the King, in the parrish
> of Tenham in Kent, being about the quantitie of seaven score
> acres : whereof he made an orchard, planting therein all those
> foraigne grafts. Which orchard is, and hath been from time to
> time, the chiefe mother of all other orchards for those kindes
> of fruites in Kent and divers other places. And afore that these
> said grafts were fetched out of Fraunce, and the Lowe Countries,
> although that there was some store of fruite in England, yet
> there wanted both rare fruite and lasting fine fruite. The Dutch
> and French finding it to be so scarce commonly plyed Billings-
> gate, especially in these countries neere London and divers
> other places, with such kinde of fruite, but now (thankes bee
> to God) divers gentlemen and others, taking delight in grafting
> . . . have planted many orchards; fetching their grafts out of
> that orchard, which Harris planted called the New-garden.

Notice that in this account pears are stated to have been
planted, whereas Lambard did not even mention them. Also
the acreage here is given as 140, as opposed to 105. In 1586,
William Camden, the antiquarian, wrote in *Britannia* :

> Then saw I Tenham . . . the parent as it were of all the choice
> fruit gardens and orchards of Kent, and the most large and
> delightsome of them all, planted in the time of King Henrie the
> Eighth by *Rich. Harris* his fruiterer, to the publique good. For
> 30 parishes thereabout are replenished with cherrie gardens and
> orchards beautifully disposed in direct lines.

A report some 100 years later shows that, though the trees were
by then just about finished, they had been very profitable in their
time. Hartlib in his *Legacie*, 1655, says :

> . . . I know in *Kent,* that some advance their ground even
> from 5s per Acre, to 5 pounds by this means (i.e. planting
> orchards), and so proportionally; and if I should relate what I
> have heard by divers concerning the profit of a *Cherry-Orchard,*

about *Sittenburn* in *Kent*, you would hardly believe me; yet I have heard it by so many, that I believe it to be true : Namely, that an *Orchard* of 30 Acres of *Cherries* produced in one year above 1000 pound, but now the Trees are almost all dead; it was one of the first *Orchards* to be planted in *Kent*. Mr Cambden reporteth, that King *Henry* the Eighth's *Gardiner* did first begin to plant *Flemish Cherries* in those parts, which in his time did spread into 32 other *Parishes*, and were at that time sold at greater rates than now : yet I know that 10, or 15 pound an acre hath been given for *Cherries*; more for *Pears* and *Apples*.

Not much is known of Richard Harris himself, but he probably had a house in Teynham parish. William Harris, thought to have been Richard's son, was a churchwarden of Teynham church at the end of the sixteenth century and gave the church its first register book. In return, it was agreed that 'the pew before the vicar's desk shall ever remayne unto him and his heirs'.

News of Harris's successful ventures into large-scale fruit growing must have spread quickly, as fruit planting started soon afterwards in many parts of the country and all sorts of people sent to the New Garden for grafts.

In 1597, the *Herball* of John Gerard was published. A barber-surgeon, Gerard was also a very keen gardener and had charge of Lord Burleigh's gardens in the Strand and at Theobalds, in Hertfordshire, as well as having a garden of his own at Holborn. He had a remarkable collection of plants and issued one of the first catalogues. About apples he says :

The fruite of Apples do differ in greatnes, forme, colour and taste; some couered with a red skin, others yellowe or greene, varying infinitely according to the soyle and climate; some very great, some little, and many of a middle sort; some are sweet of taste, or something sower; most be of a middle taste betweene sweete and sower, the which to distinguish I thinke it impossible; notwithstanding I heare of one that intendeth to write a peculiar volume of Apples, and the use of them; yet when he hath done that he can do, he hath done nothing touching their severall kindes to distinguish them.

Which seems to suggest that there was not much choice.

Nevertheless names of apples were emerging and included the following :

Pearmain : a large apple.
Reinette : from French *reine*—a little queen—or Latin *renatus*
—indicating a variety good enough for remaking, i.e. increased by grafting.
Costard : probably from *costatus*—ribbed.
Quoining : prominently ribbed.
Codlin : any small green apple.
Pippin : a seedling.

The name pearmain, as we have seen, was in use in Norfolk early in the thirteenth century but over 300 years later Parkinson, in his *Paradisus*, says that the pearmain 'differeth little either in taste or durabilitie from the pippin, and therefore next unto it is accounted the best of all apples', John Philips, the seventeenth-century poet, calls it in his *Cyder*: 'The fair Pearmain, Tempered like comeliest nymph, with red and white'. Another theory is that it owes its name to its long pear-shaped form.

The Reinette or Renate, could have been the Reinette Grise, a sixteenth-century French variety. It was yellowish green with a dull red flush covered with russet and was cultivated for several hundred years. Golden Reinette was another very old variety.

The Costard is recorded as having been on sale at Oxford in 1296, when it made 1s a hundred, and a few years later twenty-nine costard trees were sold for 3s each. A cooking apple and popular for pies, it is mentioned by most of the early horticultural writers but had almost disappeared by the end of the seventeenth century.

The Quoining, or Queening, is first heard of in Tudor times and seems to have been a name used for a whole group of apples with prominent angles or 'quoins'. Parkinson describes it as 'of two sorts, both of them great faire red apples and well relished, but the greater is the beste'. The Queene was probably another name for it.

Codlins, to begin with at least, were any small or immature green apples. But the old English codlin, with which the Kentish codlin seems to be synonymous, was cultivated as a distinct variety as early as Tudor times. It probably gets its name from being

Covent Garden in the seventeenth century.

Street market near Charing Cross.

good to 'coddle' in cooking, and lent its name to 'codlins and cream'. Parkinson describes the Kentish codlin as a 'faire great greenish apple, very good to eat when it is ripe; but the best to coddle of all apples', which leads one to suppose that it was generally used when small and green.

Though the pippin no doubt owes its names to having been raised from a seed (the French pépin), in general it seems to have stood for something rather special in dessert apples. In *Henry IV*, Justice Shallow says to Falstaff 'Nay, you shall see my orchard, where in an arbour we will eat last year's pippin of my own grafting', and Michael Drayton in *Polyolbion*, a descriptive poem of England written about 1613, says of Kent :

> Whose golden gardens seem th'Hesperides to mock
> Nor there the damson wants, nor dainty apricock,
> Nor Pippin, which we hold of kernel fruit the king.

It is probable that Richard Harris planted mostly pippins at Teynham, and they were also introduced by Leonard Mascall, who planted an orchard at Plumstead in Sussex about eight years before Harris planted his New Garden. As time went on, pippins began to develop into definite varieties. The Golden Pippin is thought to have originated at Barnham Park in Sussex and to have been exported to France as the Pippin d'Or and to Holland as the Engelsche Goud Pepping. It was golden yellow with a slight russeting.

Elizabethan literature is full of references to other apples but little is known of their origin. In *Henry IV*, Part I, Bardolph is offered 'a dish of Leathercoats', which, as the name implies, was a russet apple. Shakespeare also spoke much of the 'Apple-John' which was famous for its long keeping properties. Other names for the Apple-John were John, Densam and Winter Greening.

The Pomewater was a popular early cooking apple. According to Parkinson, it was 'an excellent good and great whitish apple, full of sap and moisture, somewhat pleasant sharpe, but a little bitter withal : it will not last long, the winter frosts soon causing it to rot and perish'.

Parkinson also mentions the Catshead, Juneating and Paradise. The Catshead, he says, 'tooke the name of the likenesse and is a

c

reasonable good apple'. Abroad it became Tête du Chat and Schafsnase. It was a large, pale yellow (when ripe) cooking apple with a faint brown flush. Philips in his *Cyder* speaks of the

> ... *Cat's Head's* weighty orb,
> Enormous in its growth, for various use
> Tho' these are meet, tho' after full repast,
> Are oft requir'd, and crown the rich dessert.

And William Ellis in *The Modern Husbandman* describes it as :

> a very useful apple to the farmer, because one of them pared and wrapped in dough serves with little trouble for making an apple dumpling, so much in request with the Kentish farmer, for being part of a ready meal, that in the cheapest manner satiates the keen appetite of the hungry ploughman, both at home and in the field, and, therefore, has now got into such reputation in Hertfordshire, and some other counties, that it is become the most common food with a piece of bacon or pickle-pork for families.

In the *Miller's Tale*, Chaucer speaks of a 'new perjenete tree'. This may have been a Juneating or Joaneting. Other known synonyms for this variety are Ginetting, Juneting, Early Jenneting, White Juneating and Primiting. It was an early-in-the-season apple, early enough perhaps in a favourable season and when grown on a south wall to warrant the name Juneating or 'June eating'. But most sources give its season as July. Dr Johnson writes it 'Gineting' in his *Dictionary* and says it is a corruption of Janeton signifying Jane or Janet. Robert Hogg in his *Fruit Manual*, however, has a different version altogether :

> My definition of the name is this. In the Middle Ages, it was customary to make the festivals of the Church periods on which occurrences were to take place or from which events were to be named. Even in the present day we hear the country people talking of some crop to be sown, or some other to be planted, at Michaelmas, St Martin's, or St Andrews tide. It was also the practice for parents to dedicate their children to some particular saint, as Jean Baptiste, on the recurrence of whose festival all who are so named keep it as a holiday. So it was also in regard to fruits, which were named after the day about which they came to maturity. Thus we have the Margaret

Apple, so called from being ripe about St Margaret's Day, the 20th of July; the Magdalene, or Maudlin, from St Magdalene's Day, the 22nd of July. And . . . we find the *Joannina*, so called, . . . because they ripened about St John's Day.

Paradise was probably the small apple used as a rootstock for some other varieties. Other apples which Harris may have planted were Pomme d'Api, Nonpareil and Sops in Wine.

Pomme d'Api, or Lady Apple, was a beautiful little dessert apple by all accounts and could be eaten from October to April. It was yellow, with a red flush on the side exposed to the sun. It has been said that it was brought from Peloponessus to Rome by Appius Claudius, but another source puts its origin as a wilding from the Forest of Api in Brittany. It may have been used by Harris under some other name, but is first mentioned in 1690 by Martin Lister who, in *A Journey to Paris*, says it is served in Paris 'for show, more than use; being a small flat apple, very beautiful red on one side, and pale or white on the other, and may serve the Ladies at their Toilet as a Pattern to paint by'. Another early writer, Worlidge, calls it 'Pomme Appease, a curious apple, lately propagated; the fruit is small and pleasant, which the Madams of France carry in their pockets, by reason they yield no unpleasant scent'.

Nonpareil is thought to have originated from seed brought out of France and planted by a Jesuit. It was pea green with some dull red and kept very well.

Sops in Wine was used both for cooking and for cider. It was a red apple going almost black where it faced the sun. Its flesh was red as if it had been 'sopped' in wine.

What pears Harris planted are difficult to ascertain as few names have been handed down. Hartlib, in his *Legacie*, says about pears:

A *friend* of mine near *Gravesend,* hath lately collected about 200 *species*. I know another in *Essex* (Mr *Ward*) who hath nigh the same number. I hear of another in *Worcestershire*, not inferiour to these. In *Northamtonshire*, I know one who hath likewise collected very many. So that I dare boldly say, there are no less in this *Island* than 5000 *species*; some commended for their early ripeness; some for excellent tastes; some for beauty; others for greatness; some for great bearers; others for good Bakers; some for long lasters; others for to make Perry, etc.

This was written some 100 years after Harris's time but no doubt he had plenty to choose from and is most likely to have planted the Bergamot, a variety which had possibly been known in Britain since Roman times. Parkinson refers to the Winter Bergamot as :

> of two or three sorts, being all of them small fruit, somewhat greener on the outside than the summer kindes; all of them very delicate and good in their due time; so some will not be fit to bee eaten when others are well-nigh spent, every of them outlasting another by a moneth or more.

Brown Beurré, a dessert pear which ripened in October, was a very old French variety also known as Beurré Gris. It was certainly grown in England in the seventeenth century if not before. Deux Têtes is mentioned by Parkinson and got its name from its two 'eyes' which seemed to divide the pear in half.

Gros Rousselt was mentioned in 1665 as being grown in England under the name of Great Russet of Remes. The Windsor pear is thought to be the English name of the French Bellissime and Suprême. Sir Hugh Platt, giving the authority of 'Master' Hill who lived about 1563, says that this pear grew on Windsor Hill, from which it derived its English name. The Bon Chrétien is also a very old pear.

Cherries are much more difficult to establish by name. Gascoigne is one of the oldest of which there is any record, and Gaskin, a corruption of Gascoigne, refers to cherries which originally came from Gascony. They are said to have been brought back from France by Joan of Kent when her husband, the Black Prince, was commanding his armies in Guienne and Gascony. The word 'Gean' often used in connection with cherries also derives from Guienne.

May Duke could be a corruption of Medoc, a district of France from which it is thought to have been obtained. It is certainly a very old variety. Carnation, with synonyms in many countries, is first mentioned in 1665 but could have been in the country a long time before that. Cluster was known to Parkinson in 1629; he called it the Flanders Cluster Cherry. Early May's origins

are lost, but as an extremely early cherry of not very high quality
it has been grown at least since records began. Parkinson also
mentions the Morello—also known as Murillo and Milan. And
the Ounce, or Tobacco-leaved, is said by Parkinson to

> have the greatest and broadest leafe of any other Cherrie, but
> beareth the smallest store of Cherries everie year, and yet
> blossometh well; the fruit also is nothing answerable to the
> name being not great, of a pale yellowish red.

The leaves of this cherry could be up to eighteen inches long.

It is difficult to know just how good the fruit was in the time
of Richard Harris. Grown in private gardens, with constant
attention by almost unlimited labour, it was possibly of a very
high standard. With 100 acres or so to look after, Harris must
have found it difficult to keep the crop clear of pests and diseases,
though the people who ate the fruit probably did not demand a
very high standard. One witness to the standard of fruit in those
days is Busoni, a chaplain to the household of the Venetian ambassador in England at the beginning of the seventeenth century.
In one of his reports to his ambassador (published in *Calendar
of State Papers (Venetian)*, 1618) he writes :

> The apples are really very good and cheap, of various sorts
> and procurable all the year round. The pears are scarcely eat-
> able and the other fruit most abominable their taste resembling
> that of insipid masticated grass. The numerous sorts of cherries
> and egriots which one sees in Italy may well be desired in this
> kingdom, though certainly not enjoyed, for generally in the
> markets they sell one single sort of very bad morella.
> Yet the English are extremely greedy of them, especially the
> women, buying them at the beginning of the season in bunches
> at the cost of an eye.
> Then these gentlewomen go with their squires to the fruit
> and flowers gardens and orchards, to strive who can eat the
> most. It occurs to me here that a few months ago a leading
> lady ate 28 pounds of this fruit in competition with a cavalier
> who was scarcely seventeen. It is true she ran the risk of her
> life, the exploit having confined her to bed for many days.

Busoni also reported that the English did not put fruit on the
table 'but between meals one sees men, women and children,
always munching through the streets, like so many goats, and

yet more in places of public amusement'. So at least there is evidence that we were eating plenty of fruit, even if our manners were not quite up to Venetian standards.

Thus by the seventeenth century, fruit growing on a commercial scale was well established in Britain and from then onwards British fruit was to be able to hold its own against all comers.

CHAPTER THREE

GARDENER CAWSWAY OF HOUNDSDITCH

A T the time when Richard Harris was planting his fruit in Kent, the city of London was growing rapidly and the supply of food had to grow with it. Until then, the surplus produce from the large gardens of the nobles, merchants, clergy and others within or just outside the city walls had been sufficient to provide all the fruit and vegetables needed. Many ordinary citizens also had small gardens in which they grew a few things for their own table. But a few keen gardeners began to find it worthwhile to buy or rent land in order to cultivate crops for sale in the market places. Little is known of these men or where they had their gardens, and many of them no doubt moved several times over the years, as one site after another was taken over for building.

John Stow's famous *Survey of London* was first published in 1598 but as Stow was then past seventy, most of the material in his book was no doubt gathered some years before this. Stow acknowledged that the model for his *Survey* was his friend William Lambard's *A Perambulation of Kent* which had appeared twenty-two years earlier. So if Stow had not been aware of the fact—unlikely in so knowledgeable a man—Lambard's book would have informed him of the new developments in commercial horticulture which Richard Harris had started with the planting of the New Garden at Teynham.

Stow does not say much about the growing of produce for sale, though market gardens certainly then existed in London. But he does mention that, in the reign of Henry VIII, three gunfounder brothers called Owen had taken over a field in Houndsditch for a foundry and that the part they did not want had been made into a garden by a gardener named Cawsway who 'served the market with herbs and roots'.

Houndsditch got its name because, in the early days, dead dogs and other rubbish were thrown into this open ditch in the city. Later, a mud wall had been built to enclose it but this attempt to discourage people from throwing things into it was never completely successful.

The field in which the Owen brothers established their foundry and Cawsway laid out his garden was owned by Magdalen College, Cambridge and, like the few other fields still left in the city, it was enclosed to prevent trespassing.

Cawsway is one of the few City of London market gardeners to be mentioned by name. And he was no doubt one of the last because, by the middle of the sixteenth century, open garden ground of any size was becoming very difficult to obtain. But many of the gardens mentioned in earlier years had almost certainly grown crops to be sold. In 1345, according to *49 Edward III Letter-Book H fol XIII*, the lease of a garden in Tower Ward, near the city wall, stated :

> unto John Watlyngtone, serjeant, a garden situate in Tower Ward, near to Londonwal, which John Scot lately held; being between the garden which Geoffrey Puppe holds, on the North side, and the garden which William Lambourne holds, on the South . . . for 30 years . . . paying 10s yearly

earlier, is said to have had over 1,000 plants in his herb garden on London Wall.

John Gerard, the famous herbalist and gardener, mentioned earlier is said to have had over 1,000 plants in his herb garden at Holborn in 1597, as well as owning another garden in Old Street. In 1602, he is reported to have been given a lease of two acres on the east side of Somerset House 'abutting on the south upon the bank or wall of the River Thames and on the north upon the back of tenements standing in the High Street called the Strand'.

The Earl of Lincoln's garden on the site of present day Lincoln's Inn Fields was also a large one. The accounts of the earl's bailiff early in the reign of Edward I show it to be growing apples, pears, nuts and cherries in quantities sufficient not only to supply the earl's table (which was a large one by all accounts) but also to provide a surplus for sale to the value of

about £150 a year in modern currency. The vegetables grown
were beans, onions, garlic and leeks. Vines and roses also featured
in the garden lists.

Up to the end of the Middle Ages, areas such as Holborn,
Finsbury, Shoreditch, Stepney, Bermondsey and Westminster
were almost entirely open country and, it is believed, largely
under cultivation. But by the time Cawsway obtained his garden,
there was not much free ground left for this purpose, though
when Houndsditch was eventually filled in, garden plots were
developed for a while on the site.

Cawsway himself was not left to enjoy his market garden for
long, and Stow reports that within a few years it was 'parcelled
into gardens wherein are now many fair houses of pleasure built'.
The fate of Cawsway's market garden was to be that of every
other that lay in the way of London's advance, though Cawsway,
like many another in the years to follow, no doubt profited from
the sale of his land and was perhaps able to set himself up again
further out of London.

Another garden mentioned by Stow and possibly used for
market crops is one at the Minories, near Tower Hill. The land
here had previously belonged to a farmer named Goodman,
but his son, says Stow, 'being heir to his father's purchase, let out
the ground first for grazing of horses and then for garden plots'
with the result that he 'lived like a gentleman thereby'. The farm
had originally belonged to a nunnery of the Order of St Clare
founded in 1293, and had been taken over by Henry VIII in
1539. It lay on the south side of the nunnery and Stow recalls
going there in his youth for 'many a halfpenny worth of milk,
and never had less than one ale quart for a halfpenny in the
winter, always hot from the kine, as the same was milked and
strained'. Goodman's Yard still preserves the name of that early
farmer whose land ran close to the City wall, on the other side
of which lay Houndsditch.

Most of the religious orders in those days had garden land.
The grounds of the Greyfriars, for example, occupied a large
corner space reaching from Newgate to St Martin's-le-Grand,
while those of St Helen's stretched from Bishopsgate Street to St
Mary Axe. The Austin Friars (Augustinian) had a garden

enclosed on one side by London Wall and covering the whole area from there to Lothbury, Broad Street and Coleman Street.

In these gardens were grown fruit, vegetables and flowers for the monks and their dependants, the surplus produce being sold in the market-places and no doubt bringing in some welcome additional revenue.

Ely Palace's forty acres of garden, orchard and vineyard on the banks of the Holborn, or Upper Fleet river, also probably contributed its share. Plum Street Court, Saffron Hill, and Vine Street were all part of the Palace gardens and bear witness to some of the crops which were grown.

The Fleet river, whose course was roughly where Farringdon Street is today was once navigable as far as Holborn bridge and, together with other small streams in London, was no doubt very useful to market gardeners until their channels became choked with refuse and had to be covered in.

By the time of Cawsway, the established gardeners were anxious to protect their reputation against the many charlatans who were foisting low-quality produce on the public. A company of 'Free Gardeners' had existed since the reign of Edward III (1327-77), but the Gardeners' Company, which received its charter in 1605, was a much more advanced form of organisation. The charter it received was for :

> the trade, craft or mystery of gardening, planting, setting, sow-ing, cutting, arboring, rocking, mounting, covering, fencing, and removing of plants, herbs, seeds, fruits, trees, stocks, sets, and of contriving the conveyances to the same belonging.

According to a petition they sent to the Lord Mayor :

> . . . they can hurte no Companie in London, for theire Life is altogether in the ffieldes or Gardens. And so desirous of Libertie and Ayer, that they will not be tied to a Shopp, nor, are they capeable of anie other trade.

They also informed the Lord Mayor that it was they who took away, 'the dung and noysommes of the cittie' and

> . . . imploye thousandes of poore people, ould men, women and children, in sellinge of their Commodities, in weedinge, in

gatheringe of Stones Etc, which would be otherwise verie
burdensome to the cittie, and suburbes thereof.

The first master of the Gardeners' Company was Thomas
Young, and the first wardens were John Markham and Thomas
Morrall. The Company of Fruiterers was formed a few months
later, with John Stanley as master and James Sawle and William
Clarke as wardens.

The early records of both companies mention gardens within
the city, as well as many more just outside, but as the name
'market garden' had not yet come into use, it is often impossible
to tell which were private gardens and which were not. One may
assume, however, that the mention of their names in the report
of a trade association indicates that their owners were in the
industry for profit.

The professional gardeners had to struggle all the time against
competition from private gardeners, as well as against those who
came into the business with little knowledge and often spoiled
the good name of the industry. This problem was to be always
with them. As late as 1726, Richard Bradley was writing in *A
General Treatise of Husbandry and Gardening* :

> within the Memory of Men now living, *Somerset House*, and
> the Buildings thereabouts, were styled Country-houses, and the
> open Places about them were employ'd in Gardens for Profit;
> and many parts now within the City and Liberties, were then
> in the Possession of working Gardeners, who were at that Time
> enough in number; and employ'd Ground enough to furnish
> the Town with Garden Necessaries, for then there were few
> Herbs used at the Table with regard to what there are now;
> but the Success which those regular Gardeners met with at that
> Time, encourag'd many others to set up and profess the same
> Calling near *London*, who so unskilfully went to work, that
> many abuses were committed, and the Subject was injur'd by
> them. . . .

One of the stated reasons for the setting up of the Company
of Gardeners was to 'inspect the Worth of others, who tended
to practise without Knowledge, or should offer to invade their
Customs'. The Company tried hard to keep outsiders away :

> we . . . prohibit and forbid that no Person or Persons whatso-
> ever, inhabiting within the said City of *London* . . . or within

six miles compass of that same City, do at any Time hereafter use or exercise the Art or Mystery of Gardening . . . without the Licence and Consent of the Company.

They also laid down where the produce was to be sold :

> . . . no Person or Persons being not admitted of the said Company and dwelling above the space of six Miles from the said City of *London*, shall from henceforth sell or put to sale any Plants, Herbs, Roots, Seeds, Trees, Stocks, Slips, Sets, Flowers or other things sold by Gardeners . . . only in and at such accustomed Times and places as the Foreign Baker, and other Foreigners, being not free of our said City, use to do with their Bread and other Victuals. . . .

The master and wardens had full power to seize goods and, if they were not of high enough quality, to destroy them.

Cawsway may have sold his produce by St Paul's churchyard at a time when the cathedral was just recovering from a bad phase in its history. Since the Middle Ages, it had become common practice to treat the cathedral as a place people could walk through, and even as a market place where pilgrims bought badges and souvenirs from stalls which were set up in the body of the church itself. There were also professional letterwriters and the like. In 1385, the 'playing of ball' was forbidden within the cathedral and even in Cawsway's time the Common Council of London had to step in and forbid, among other things, the leading of horses and mules through the cathedral.

Towards the end of the sixteenth century, the central aisle, Paul's Walk, had become the greatest promenade in London and it was said that more business was done there than in the Royal Exchange. In 1561, according to Henry Machin in his *Diary* 'someone maid a fray in Powles Church' for which that 'someone' was nailed by his ear to a post in the churchyard and afterwards had the ear cut off.

In 1659, it was reported by the Gardeners' Company :

> that the markett lately kept in Saint Paules Churchyard for fruites, flowers, hearbes, roots, plants and other Commodytes was ordered to be removed into Aldersgate Street and Broad Street which increaseth ye trouble and charge of ye incorporated Gardiners and other Country people that bring their Commodytes by water, by reason of ye farther distance of ye place

from ye waterside. That now the whole resort is to Aldersgate street (being more convenient than Broad Street) by means thereof ye said incorporated Gardiners and others coming from ye waterside are disturbed and disordered and many times disappointed of their usual standing in ye said marketts by Costermongers, Haglers, Ingrossers, Fforestallers and other rude people that frequent and encroach upon ye said m'kett and claime as much Freedom there as ye Gardiners and Country people for whose accomdacon and incouragment to supply this Citty with sweet and wholesome Commodytes ye said markett was intended. . . .

So the market outside St Paul's must have gone sometime at the beginning of the seventeenth century.

Possibly Cawsway sold at Gracechurch Street, which was not far from his market garden. For the 'Hearb Markett in Gracious street . . . is an auncient Markett and very convenient for the people that dwell in the East part of this City'.

A number of small street markets would also, as today, have sold vegetables and fruit. One is mentioned by Stow as being on the south side of Cheapside; this would lead up to the market at St Paul's. Here were houses, according to Stow, that were 'of old time but shedds where a woman sold seeds, roots, and herbs . . . by encrochment on ye high street'. Perhaps this woman was the one mentioned by Henry Machin as being in the pillory for giving short weight.

The furst day of July (1552) ther was a man and a woman on the pelere in Chepe-syd; the man sold potts of straberries, the whyche the pott was nott alff fulle, but fyllyed with forne (fern).

No wonder the Gardeners' Company was worried about its image!

The range of vegetables sold could not have been very extensive. Many were still only being used in soups. Andrew Boorde in *A Compendyous Regyment, or a Dyetary of Helth, 1542*, says : 'Potage is not so moch vsed in al Crystendom as it is vsed in Englande' and mentions in particular 'pease potage' and 'bean potage'. He also mentions that fennel was in great demand for flavouring soups.

John Gerard, writing in 1597, says that there were two types of turnip in cultivation (and possibly a third one with red roots which he had not seen). One of the varieties grew particularly well in a sandy soil at Hackney 'a village near London'. He adds that these Hackney-grown turnips were brought 'to the Crosse in Cheapside by the women of that village to be solde, and are the best that ever I tasted'.

In 1586 Virginian potatoes, as they were then called, were just becoming known, though a sweet potato had been introduced some time before. Gerard, in his *Herball*, comments that sweet potatoes were eaten :

> rosted in the ashes; some, when they be so rosted, infuse them, and sop them in wine; and others to give them the greater grace in eating, do boil them with prunes and so eat them. And likewise others dresse them (being first rosted) with oile, vinegar, and salt, every man according to his own taste and liking; notwithstanding howsoever they be dressed, they comfort, nourish and strengthen the bodie.

These sweet potatoes were most probably those which John Hawkins brought back from his voyage to the 'coast of Guinea and the Indies of Nova Hispania' in 1564. Richard Hakluyt in *The Principall Navigations of the English Nation* some twenty years afterwards describes them as 'the most delicate rootes that may be eaten, and doe farre exceed our passeneps or carets'.

The Virginian potato, *Solanum tuberosum*, was a luxury to begin with, ranking with the date and the orange as a rarity. Dawson in his *Good Housewife's Jewel*, published in 1596, treats it as a leading ingredient of a tart :

> Take two quinces, and two or three burre rootes and a *Potaton*, and pare your *Potaton* and scrape your roots, and put them into a quart of wine, and let them boyle till they bee tender, and put in an ounce of dates, and when they be boiled tender, drawe them through a strainer, wine and all, and then put in the yolkes of eight eggs, and the braynes of three or four cocke-sparrowes, and strain them into the other, and a little rose-water, and seeth them all with sugar, cinnamon, and ginger, and cloves, and mace; and put in a little sweet butter, and set it upon a chafing-dish of coles between two platters, to let it boyle till it be something bigge.

Its introduction has been attributed to both Sir Francis Drake

and Sir Walter Raleigh. But whoever introduced it, the potato
came into its own a century later when it was grown as a cheap
form of food. John Forster issued a pamphlet in 1664 with the
long title *England's happiness increased: or, a sure and easie
remedy against all succeeding dear years; by a plantation of the
roots called potatoes, etc. etc. By which ten thousand men in
England and Wales, who know not how to live, or what to do
to get a maintenance for their families, may of one acre of ground
make thirty pounds per annum. Invented and published for the
good of the poorer sort. By John Forster, Gent., London.*

Forster's idea was for the king to import seed potatoes from
Ireland and to licence a certain number of people to grow them—
each being given one bushel. This scheme did not succeed but
many more potatoes were produced.

Artichokes were also popular around this time. Busoni, the
chaplain to the Venetian ambassador, who did not like the way
the English ate their apples, had a good word to say for the
artichoke. He described them as :

> beautiful and fine-flavoured artichokes, of a sort different from
> ours, that is to say much larger and of a reddish tinge. Of these
> they gather an immense quantity during 10 months of the year
> and sell them at a very cheap rate.

Busoni was also impressed by our cabbages. He claims to have
seen some weighing 35 lb the pair, and says that his ambassador
had actually come across one single cabbage weighing 28 lb.

In another report, Busoni says that England was very gravelly
to a depth of six to seven feet so that, unless aided by industry,
the soil would yield no vegetables or very few 'especially in the
environs of London where they are needed'. It was the custom
in England, he said, to dig up the gravel which was then used
for ballast in the ships or for repairing streets and to fill the space
to a depth of four or five feet with the 'filth of the city'. This
'filth' served as an excellent manure 'rich and black as thick ink'.
The manure was brought by the street carts and the result,
according to Busoni, was that :

> In a very short while many spots are improved and fertilised,
> their proprietors enclosing them immediately for their safe
> custody, in various ways at small cost. Some effect this by

means of palings; others sink very deep ditches, some again
form the enclosure of soft mud mixed with half rotten straw
and this being raised to a sufficient height from the ground,
they surmount it with a thatch of rye straw which serves for
eaves. On the top of this thatch, which projects a foot on either
side they place a parapet of mud, to consolidate the eaves and
preserve this mud structure which soon becomes very hard.

John Tradescant, Senior.

John Tradescant, Junior.

The Tradescant cherry

Horticultural tools of various periods—from a collection in Yorkshire.

CHAPTER FOUR

SEEDSMAN CHILD OF PUDDING LANE

THE greater interest being shown in the cultivation of choice plants meant that someone had to provide the seeds of these newer and better varieties. From time immemorial, gardeners had collected seed from selected plants and used it for themselves or favoured neighbours. By the sixteenth century, however, the selling of seed had become a business. Most of the early seedsmen had their headquarters in London, where the seed they had either grown themselves or had grown for them was collected, packed in convenient quantities and sold to gardeners throughout the land. From these humble beginnings rose many of the famous seed houses.

To provide the seeds and plants for market gardeners such as Cawsway, and for the gardeners of the noblemen and gentry, stalls in the street markets were first set up and small shops soon followed. The proprietors of these no doubt purchased the seed of promising plants brought to their notice by gardeners and either grew larger quantities of it themselves or had it grown for them by gardeners or farmers who had land in particularly good areas for seed production.

The range of seed required had become very wide by the middle of the sixteenth century. Thomas Tusser, whose first edition of *500 Points of Good Husbandry* was published in 1557, gives lists of plants and seeds to be cultivated during the twelve months of the year. He lists forty-two herbs for kitchen use and another twenty-two for salads and sauces. Under 'Herbs and Roots, to boil or to butter' he gives beans, carrots, cabbages, parsnips, rape, turnip, peas, pumpkins, radishes, gourds and 'citrons'.

Fruits mentioned by him include apples, apricots, barberries, bullaces, cherries, chestnuts, plums, damsons, filberts, gooseberries, grapes, hurtleberries, medlars, mulberries, peaches, pears, 'pear plums', quinces, raspberries, strawberries, and walnuts. The raspberry and gooseberry were evidently fairly new introductions for, in his hints for September, Tusser in his quaint rhyme prose says :

> The Barberry, Respis and Gooseberry too
> Looke now to be planted as other things doo,
> The Gooseberry, Respis, and Roses, all three
> With Strawberries under them trimly agree.

One man who set out to cater for this demand was a Mr Child, whose premises in 1560 were in Pudding Lane where a hundred or so years later the Great Fire of London was to start. When Child started, many new plants were being imported from distant countries, among them being the tobacco plant brought into England by Sir John Hawkins in 1565. Its narcotic properties for smoking and snuff-taking were quickly recognized and its popularity was frowned upon by many people. King James I, for example, in his *Counterblast to Tobacco*, called its use :

> a custom loathsome to the eye, hateful to the nose, harmful to the brain, dangerous to the lungs, and in the black stinking fume thereof nearest resembling the horrible Stygian smoke of the pit that is bottomless.

Despite the king's and other people's strong disapproval, the habit grew and no doubt Child at his Pudding Lane shop sold plenty of *Nicotiana tabacum* to gardeners wishing to try and grow their own tobacco.

But the range of common herbs would have formed the greatest part of his trade. Every sixteenth-century book on gardening devoted most of its space to herbs, which were wanted not only for medicinal purposes but also for improving (or masking) the flavour of much of the food that was served. Another wide use for herbs was for sweetening the atmosphere, for which purpose they could either be carried or the floor strewn with them. Nosegays are still carried at the ceremonies of the presentation of the Royal Maundy money and at the installation of the Lord Mayor of London.

A wide range was classified as medicinal. Even such plants as lettuce came into this category and, eaten with salt and oil, it was recommended for cooling the blood. According to Thomas Hill in *The Profitable Art of Gardening*, lettuce 'if plucked up by the roots, with the left hand, before the sun rising, and the same laid under the coverings of the bed, the sick body not knowing thereof . . .' would help people to sleep soundly. But, says Hill, it should not be given to expectant mothers or the offspring would be 'far unlike their fathers in that they shall be both rageing in minde and foolish in wit'.

Child in his Pudding Lane shop would also have kept a wide range of flower seeds such as wallflowers, violets, stocks, sweet williams, columbines, campions, cowslips, hollyhocks, marigolds, pansies, pinks, snapdragons—all of which are still grown today. And no doubt he had bulbs of snowdrops, daffodils and even the tulip which, though expensive, was becoming popular.

Certainly he would have had a collection of roses; for even in the sixteenth century the rose was already the most popular flower in England. Favourite was the sweet-scented double red *Rosa gallica*, followed closely by *Rosa alba*, the white rose. Others were the cabbage rose and red Provence (*R. centifolia*), damask (*R. damascena*), *R. mundi* with its striped red and white petals, the musk (*R. moschata*) and the cinnamon (*R. cinnamomea*).

The red and white roses came into prominence during the Wars of the Roses when they identified the two parties. Shakespeare in *Henry VI* says:

> This brawl today,
> Grown to this faction in the Temple-garden,
> Shall send between the red rose and the white
> A thousand souls to death and deadly night.

Spenser, in his *Ditty in Praise of Eliza, Queen of the Shepherds*, mentions several of the more popular flowers of the age, giving their everyday names.

> Bring hether the Pincke and purple Cullambine
> With Gilliflowers;
> Bring Coronations, and Sops-in-wine
> Worn of Paramoures;
> Strow me the ground with Daffodowndillies,

And Cowslips, and Kingcups, and lovèd Lillies;
The pretie Pawnce,
And the Chevisaunce,
Shall match with the fayre flower Delice.

(Gilliflowers were probably pinks; coronations, carnations; sops-in-wine, carnations or pinks; pawnces, pansies; chevisaunces, wallflowers; while flower delice was probably the iris.)

When Child set up his shop, gardens were beginning to be much improved, not only as regards the range of flowers, trees and herbs but also in colour and size. It was an age of discovery and the ships which went to countries such as America and the West Indies brought back seeds and plants previously unknown.

On the continent of Europe, particularly in France and the Low Countries, horticulture was still far in advance of England. In Flanders, for example, gardening had reached a high level of development as early as the fourteenth century, and by the sixteenth century, onions were being exported in considerable quantities. Those destined for England came mostly to the dock at Queenhithe, not far from Child's shop, and no doubt onion sets and seeds, as well as many other seeds, reached him by this route.

The Flemish Protestant refugees who arrived at Sandwich and other coast towns in the second half of the sixteenth century to spread their ideas of horticulture also sold seed and must have been responsible for many new introductions.

Samuel Hartlib in his *Legacie* says that :

> Some old men of *Surrey*, where it (the *Art of Gardening*) flourisheth very much at present, report, that they knew the first *Gardiners* that came into those parts, to plant *Cabbages*, *Colleflowers* and to sowe *Turneps*, *Carrets*, and *Parsnips* and to sow *Raith* (early) *Peas*, all of which at that time were great rarities, he having few or none in England but what came from Holland and Flaunders.

By 1591, onions are reported to have been growing on the fen soils of Lincolnshire and, again, this may have been the work of Flemish refugees who are known to have gone to this area. The onions and other vegetables were sold in the markets of Stourbridge and Peterborough, both very important at that time.

Besides his London customers, Child would have had people buy from him from all parts of the country. Perhaps William Darrell of Littlecote, Wiltshire, who 'paid a Dutch gardiner and kept him lavishly supplied with seeds and plants' went to him. He certainly went to London for his tools as one of his accounts (quoted by H. Hall in *Society in the Elizabethan Age*) includes 'carriage of garden tools from London 2s'. Other items in Darrell's accounts are:

Gardening stuffe for Cornelius the gardener	23s	3d
Garden seeds	3s	3d
Garden seeds	4s	7d
Rosemary		10d
Strawberries		9d

A bill paid by Queen Elizabeth for flowers to welcome the City trained bands who entertained her with a military display is still preserved at Greenwich:

Gely flowers and marygolds	1s	3d
Garland		7d
Strawing herbs	1s	4d
Bowes for the chemneys		1d
Flowers for the potts in the wyndowes		6d

Queen Elizabeth's favourite 'strawing herb' for spreading on the floors was meadow sweet.

A hundred years later, we find a descendant of Child still in the seed business, though we do not know whether he was in Pudding Lane. If he was, he must have been rudely awakened on that night in September 1666 when fire broke out at the near-by shop of Farynor, the king's baker.

Pudding Lane had got its name, according to Stow, because 'the butchers of Eastcheap have their scalding house for hogs there, and their puddings, with other filth of beasts, are voided down that way to their dung boats in the Thames'.

Perhaps the early Child also did business in supplying dung to market gardeners who were beginning to take big supplies from the London streets for gardens and farms. Pudding Lane was also known as Rother Lane or Red Rose Lane. Red Rose suggests it was at one time horticultural land and though Stow says that, in his time, it was chiefly inhabited by basket-makers, turners and butchers, he reports several gardens in the vicinity, particularly a large one belonging to Sir John Philpot.

By the time of the Great Fire, Pudding Lane consisted of tottering timber houses and was so narrow that a cart could hardly get through. The tops of the houses almost touched across the street. The shop and house of Farynor, the king's baker, was ten doors from Thames Street. The fire probably started in one of his ovens but it was an hour or so before it really got going and reached the next house. So Child, if he were there, would possibly have had time to save most of his precious seeds. Once the fire was under way there was no stopping it, especially when the big sheds and warehouses down by the River Thames were reached. Samuel Pepys saw the fire as he got up that September morning and recorded it in his diary :

> By and by Jane comes and tells me that she hears that above 300 houses have been burned down tonight by the fire we saw, and that it is now burning down all Fish Street, by London Bridge. So I made myself ready presently, and walked to the Tower; and there got up me upon one of the high places . . . and did see the house at that end of the bridge all on fire. So down, with my heart full of trouble, to the Lieutenant of the Tower, who tells me that it began this morning in the King's Baker's house in Pudding Lane. . . .

Queenhithe, then an important dock with a market place alongside, soon burnt out. So did Gracechurch Street which had a market for herbs and fruit and was where Cawsway may have sold his produce in earlier days. Burnt out, too, was the Stocks market, another favourite resort, as we have seen, of London's market gardeners.

People fleeing from the flames took their belongings to the nearest open spaces away from the conflagration. Places such as Lincoln's Inn Fields, Gray's Inn Fields, Hatton Garden and Covent Garden's new piazza (then just developing as a fruit and vegetable market) were filled with goods.

Dryden, who was living at this time, wrote in *Annus Mirabilis* :

> Those who have homes, when home they do repair
> To a last lodging call their wandering friends :
> Their short uneasy sleeps are broke with care,
> To look how near their own destruction tends :

The most in fields like herded beast lie down,
To dews obnoxious on the grassy floor;
And while their babes in sleep their sorrows drown,
Sad parents watch the remnants of their store.

After the Great Fire, Child is lost for a while so far as the records go, but the family appears to have kept on the seed business as the name reappears as Field & Child in 1810. Field is thought to have started about the same time as Child but all we know about him is that he was J. Field and became J. & J. Field in 1771. In 1810, the two joined forces to become Field & Child and the first of a long series of amalgamations and takeovers had begun. The story of these is worth recording here as it is typical of what happened to many other seed merchants over the years.

Somewhere around 1850, Field & Child were united with Beck & Henderson and the combined business was carried on as Beck, Henderson & Child, first in the Strand, then in the Adelphi Terrace, and lastly at Upper Thames Street. The firm of Beck, which specialised in choice strains of most garden and farm seeds, had started at the close of the seventeenth century and towards the end of the first Mr Beck's life he became associated with a Robert Allan, the business being known for many years as Beck & Allan. On the retirement of Allan, Henderson joined the firm. He died in 1868, and when, in 1870, George Child, the surviving partner, disposed of the business to Waite, Burnell & Co, the old name disappeared. Thus members of the Child family had remained in the business for over 300 years.

The new firm of Waite, Burnell & Co who took over from the Childs were no newcomers to the business, being successors of J. G. Waite, who had been a market gardener and seed grower in Camberwell. As his seed business increased, Waite gave up his market garden and moved to Hatton Garden where he set himself up as a seedsman proper. Later he went to High Holborn. At his death his stepson, who had worked with him, entered into partnership with the firm of Huggins & Taylor and the firm became Waite, Burnell, Huggins & Company and moved to 79, Southwark Street.

The next famous seeds name to come into the business is that of Minier. The first record of a Minier is in the early part of the eighteenth century at 'Ye Signe of the Orange Tree', No 60, Strand. Here the Miniers carried on a thriving business, particularly with the gardeners using the nearby Covent Garden market, which by now was the most important in London. They stayed here for over 100 years, though there were various amalgamations including at least five changes in name between 1781 and 1799. Many of the amalgamations were probably with seed growers who were brought into the firm on agreeing to produce the seeds required.

A partner in 1871 was a man named Mason, but he seems to have fallen out with his partners and set up a rival establishment at the 'Sign of the Orange Tree', 152 Fleet Street, the similarity of names no doubt leading to some confusion. Two years after setting up on his own, John Mason issued a catalogue (he may have published one before but it has not been found) the title page of which reads :

> Fine Double Hyacinth and other various Flower Roots and Seeds, Imported chiefly from Holland, France, America, Italy, Botany Bay etc, by John Mason, Orange Tree, 152 Fleet Street.

Meanwhile, the Miniers continued in business with names such as Teesdale, Oliver, Fair and Nash coming into the business title. Nash, for example, was a miller and seed grower of Biggleswade. In 1880, the Minier concern joined forces with the firm which Child had started and, seven years later, it was incorporated with Cooper Taber.

Cooper Taber themselves had been formed from several small companies or individual seedsmen, the earliest being J. Wrench of 1750 and Edward Cross of 1771. The first Cooper comes into the picture as being connected with the Mason concern which set up at the 'Sign of the Orange Tree' in Fleet Street. In 1867, Robert Cooper became sole proprietor of this concern and carried on the business under his own name until, with the expiration of the lease in Fleet Street, he moved to Southwark Street. A few years after his death, his firm joined forces with Taber & Cullen, seed growers, at Rivenhall, Essex, to form Cooper, Taber & Co. At the same time the firm of Hy. Clarke was incorporated.

Another seedsman who amalgamated after a good many years

on his own was George Charlwood. In 1834, Charlwood was issuing a seed catalogue from premises in Tavistock Row, Covent Garden and shortly afterwards he was in business as Charlwood & Cummings in Hart Street and the adjoining James Street, Covent Garden, until eventually selling out to William Watkins in 1871. Watkins later joined Cooper Taber.

None of these firms would have grown all their own seeds. The most favoured places for seed raising tended to be to the east of the country where the climate is driest, though in the eighteenth century Battersea was noted for its cabbage seed and Deptford for its onions. Outside London, Saffron Walden acquired a reputation for chervil, radish and cress, Kent for peas, Norfolk for turnips, Lincolnshire for rape and Durham for mustard. In many of these places the seed would have been grown by seed farmers and either sold privately by sample to the seedsmen or put on sale in the seed markets such as Mark Lane in London or in country markets.

If a nursery man or market gardener raised a particularly good strain of something, he could send the seed to one of these seed farmers to grow on in bigger quantities. It was then grown, ripened and cleaned at a fixed price.

In April 1843, an advertisement in the horticultural trade press was headed :

NEW HORTICULTURAL AND AGRICULTURAL SEED ESTABLISHMENT,
6, LEADENHALL STREET.

and continued :

William Hurst and William George McMullen for many years engaged in the house of Warner & Warner, 28, Cornhill, beg respectfully to acquaint their Friends and the Public that, circumstances having arisen which induced them to leave the service of that establishment they commenced Business as Wholesale and Retail SEEDSMEN and FLORISTS at the above-named premises on Monday, the 13th inst., and they can confidently assure all who may kindly favour them with orders, that from the numerous resources they possess, through an extensive connexion with the best Seed Growers, both in this country and on the continent, and from many years practical experience in the various branches of the Business, they are enabled to offer every article of first-rate, genuine quality, and no exertion will be spared to give prompt attention to every order, and endeavouring to merit a continuance of their support.

A short list of what they had to offer followed, and included collections of asters, zinnias, balsams, hollyhocks and larkspur 'from the first German growers known', and plants such as Myatt's New British Queen strawberries (10s 6d per 100) and

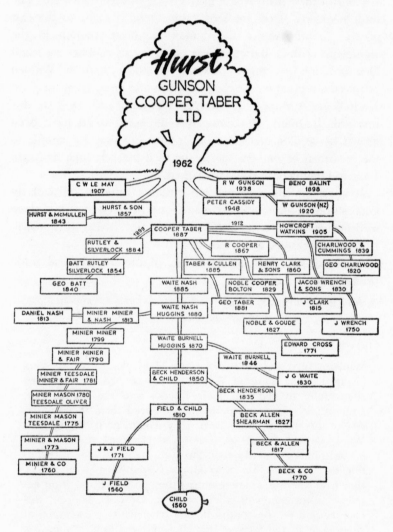

Family tree of Hurst, Gunson, Cooper Taber Ltd, Seedsmen.

Grayson's Giant asparagus (3s per 100). Seeds were priced at 6d and 1s per packet (common varieties 3d per packet.) Their earliest trial grounds were at Croydon but these were later moved to Chelmsford in Essex.

A few years after this, McMullen left to set up on his own at Hertford, and when William Hurst Junior joined his father the firm became Hurst & Son. Nathaniel Sherwood joined the firm in 1862, and eventually took full control. The firm continued to trade under the name of Hurst and was destined to reach the forefront of the seed world. In 1954, it took over the firm of Gunson, which had originated in New Zealand. In 1962, Hurst and Cooper Taber joined forces; at the same time Le May, Cassidy and Bellint came in and the whole concern set up business at Witham in Essex under the name of Hurst Gunson Cooper Taber.

Thus from Mr Child's small shop in Pudding Lane in 1560 has stemmed one of today's giants in the seed business. But in principle, the business has remained the same—the provision of clean, true-to-type seeds of a wide range of varieties.

CHAPTER FIVE

JOHN TRADESCANT OF LAMBETH

IT was comparatively easy to sell seeds and plants, but very much more difficult to obtain new varieties. At first, most seeds came from plants discovered in English gardens or brought over by invading armies and it was not until travel on the Continent became easier that any great progress was made. Once the professional gardeners were able to travel abroad they were in a position to recognize and select the best new plants.

Professional gardeners became in great demand during the Tudor period and the best among them wielded considerable power. Royalty and nobility were proud of their gardens and vied with one another in producing newer and better flowers, vegetables and fruits. It was they who first started sending their gardeners abroad to see what they could find.

In south London, a little way from the Oval cricket ground, is Tradescant Road. It is now part of a heavily built-up area and few people give a thought as to how it got its name. Yet it is a name famous in the history of horticulture.

John Tradescant was born in London towards the end of the sixteenth century but little else is known about him until his marriage to Elizabeth Day at Meopham in Kent in 1607. It is believed that he was then working as a gardener at nearby Shorne, a manor belonging to the Earl of Salisbury. What is certain, however, is that soon after his marriage he went to Hatfield House in Hertfordshire, the home of the Earl of Salisbury, where he was made responsible for planning and laying out the gardens.

A keen gardener himself, the earl soon sent Tradescant abroad to find new plants and trees, and documents in the Hatfield archives show how he travelled, what he collected and how he laid out his money. In 1611, after first spending three days at the earl's London house preparing for the trip, he took ship for

Flushing. He went off to a bad start for, after leaving Gravesend, his ship was forced into Ramsgate harbour because of high winds and he did not reach Flushing until four days later.

From Flushing he went to Leyden, where he bought 'strange and rare' shrubs and flowers. Then to Haarlem, where he visited nurseryman Cornellis Helin and bought :

> 32 rathe ripe cherries at 4s each; 1 Spanish pear 2s; 1 apple quince 3s; 1 rathe ripe cherry 3s; 2 mulberries 6s; 6 messenger trees 3s; 6 red currants 1s; 2 arborvita trees 1s; anemones 5s; 16 province roses 8s.

The rathe ripe (early) cherry is probably the Early Flanders mentioned by John Parkinson in his *Paradisus*. The messenger tree is mezereon, *Daphne mezereum*.

While at Haarlem, Tradescant also visited Cornellis Cornellison and bought narcissi and fritillaries. Then on to Delft to see Dirryk Hevesson for cherries, quinces, medlars, apples, white currants and tulips, as well as to buy two baskets and two scythes.

From Delft, Tradescant went on to Rotterdam, Antwerp and Brussels. In Brussels, he visited John Buret who sold him :

> 4 great Creeke cherries at 4s each; 6 long speckled cherries at 4s; 2 lat ripe cherries at 5s; 3 gratiola pears at 4s; 1 portingall pear at 4s; 2 Dorns pears at 2s 6d; 5 rathe ripe cherries at 2s 6d; 1 boores cherry (excedying great) 12s; 1 whit aprycoke 6s.

He also bought peaches, pears, tulips, and walnut trees.

The 'excedying great Cherye called the boores Cherye' which he bought from John Buret was possibly the cherry later known as Tradescant's Heart which, in Kent today, is still regarded as a separate variety though in other districts it is a synonym for the Noble.

Next nurseryman to be visited was John Jokkat, from whom Tradescant ordered 100 cherry trees and some flowers. He then went on to Paris, where he was introduced to Jean Robin, the famous gardener to the French royal family. Robin provided him with pomegranate, orange, oleander, myrtle, fig, and 'genista hispanyca'. For one-year-old orange trees in pots, he had to pay 10s each.

At Rouen, he visited Lamont, from whom he bought more

trees and plants while waiting for his other purchases at French nurseries to arrive. His Dutch and Belgian purchases had already been sent home and, once the French purchases were safe aboard ship at Rouen, Tradescant rode on horseback to Dieppe to take the short route to England.

Travelling was far from being easy in the seventeenth century. Even after arriving at a south coast port, Tradescant had to go by horseback to Canterbury and from there to Gravesend where the ship with his goods was awaiting him. In London, he had to arrange for the cargo to be taken by smaller boat up the River Lea as near as possible to Hatfield. It was no small operation as the consignment from France alone contained 500 trees as well as a wide assortment of plants, bulbs, seeds and tools. And the combined Dutch and Belgian consignment was almost as large.

The planting of these trees and plants must have kept Trades-cant busy for quite a while, and when it was done he had to turn his attention to the gardens of Salisbury House in the Strand. This town house had been rather neglected compared with Hat-field House, and as roses were its main theme, Tradescant once more had to go to France. This time he returned with a wonderful assortment which included twenty standard white, 800 sweet briar and 600 long briar.

Somewhere about this time Tradescant decided to go into the farming business, though only as a sideline. He persuaded the earl to rent him fifty-nine acres, which included thirty-two acres of woodland. On this land he had a small croft where he no doubt raised a few special plants of his own.

Possibly Tradescant also possessed land in Kent, for he still owned his house at Meopham. He ceased working for the Cecil family at Hatfield House about 1615 and his next post was with Sir Edward Wotton at St Augustine's Palace, Canterbury, a large house which had been used as a royal palace by Henry VIII.

In 1618, Sir Dudley Digges of nearby Barham was sent by the king on a trade mission to Russia and Tradescant received per-mission to go with him to see what he could find in the way of new plants. The mission was a failure for everyone except Tradescant, who returned with a valuable load of all kinds of plants. He also brought back in his notebook the first known list of Russian plants, with remarks about them. He did not think much of the Russian strawberries 'nothing differing from ours, but only less', but the currants were 'whit, red and black, far greatter than ever I have seen in this cuntrie'.

His most important discovery was the common larch, which was to become one of Britain's leading timber trees. He also brought back curiosities for a 'museum' he was beginning to assemble. These included the Gorara or Colymbus bird; Russian, Muscovey and Lapland boots; iron-shod Russian snowshoes and the Duke of Muscovy's vest 'wrought with gold upon the breast and arms'. From Greenland, he obtained shoes, boots, stockings and a coat made from the 'intrails of fishes'.

Tradescant's next trip was as a 'gentleman adventurer' in an expedition against the Algerian corsairs. He had heard of a wonderful golden apricot to be found in Algiers and managed to obtain permission from his employer to join the expedition. An English fleet under Sir Robert Mansell set sail from Plymouth and Tradescant followed close behind in the pinnace *Mercury*, captained by Phineas Pett, Commissioner of the Navy. No one seems to have known just what the expedition was supposed to accomplish but little harm seems to have been done to any of the pirates. What Tradescant did is also rather vague but the *Mercury* was away from Britain for seven months and called in at many places around the Mediterranean where Tradescant was able to go ashore and search for new plants.

He seems to have found his golden 'Barbarie apricoke' as well as several new plums and peaches. One important find was the 'corn flagge of Constantinople', which grew by the acre in north Africa and which we know as the gladiolus.

Tradescant also added to his collection of curiosities in the form of shoes and spurs from Barbary, a Moor's cap, chains from Spain, a knife from Damascus and a vest from Arabia. There was also an 'orange gathered from a tree that grew over Zebulon's Tombe'. (This tomb was in the Holy Land but there is nothing to show that Tradescant travelled as far as this.) There were also other items from Turkey but these and the orange from the Holy Land may have been sold to him by other travellers.

In 1625, John Tradescant became gardener to the Duke of Buckingham at Newhall in Essex. In his *Diary*, Evelyn describes Newhall in 1656 as:

a faire old house built with brick, low, being only of 2 stories, as the manner then was; the Gate-house better; the Court large and pretty; the staire-case of extraordinary widenesse, with a piece representing *Sir F. Drake's action* in the year 1580, an excellent sea-piece; the galleries are trifling; the hall is noble; the garden a faire plot, and the whole seate well accommadated with water; but above all I admir'd the faire avenue planted with stately lime-trees in 4 rowes, for neere a mile in length. It has three descents, which is the only fault, and may be reform'd. There is another faire walk of the same at the mall and wildernesse, with a tennis-court, and pleasant terrace towards the park, which was well stor'd with deere and ponds.

Most of the garden lay-out and the 'faire avenue planted with stately lime-trees' was probably Tradescant's handiwork, as he was given the task of redesigning the gardens.

When he took this job, he gave up his house at Meopham and moved to London, or rather to a part of Surrey that was later to become London. This was Lambeth, where he took a house in the grounds of Caron House, owned by the Dean and Chapter of Canterbury.

By this time Tradescant was considerably more than a gardener; he was a director of gardens and already famous for his work in introducing new trees and plants from abroad. About this time, the Duke of Buckingham gave him the position of 'garnetter' at Whitehall, a term which stems from a period when rural life in England was disrupted by the Enclosure Acts and agriculture had swung over extensively to sheep farming. Corn was at certain times in short supply and, to help feed the people in towns, granaries were built where it could be stored after a good season to help ease the price if a bad season followed. Tradescant's job was to look after the London granaries. But by the time he took the post, it had become more or less of a sinecure and was a reward for the good work he was doing.

In 1627, Tradescant went abroad again, this time with the Earl of Buckingham's expedition to liberate La Rochelle. After an impressive start, things went wrong, but despite the severe

Strawberry girl crying her wares,
about 1800.

Flower girl in a London street,
about 1900.

Covent Garden in the eighteenth century.

fighting Tradescant seems to have been able to carry on with his search for new plants as he came back with the scarlet corn poppy, *Papaver rhoeas* (from which the Shirley poppy was afterwards developed), and the stock, *Matthiola sinuata* (from which came the ten weeks stock). He also collected several more items for his museum.

Tradescant reached the peak of his career in 1630 when he was appointed Keeper of His Majesty's Gardens, Vines and Silkworms at Oatland at a salary of £100 a year. Oatland—the district is now known as Oatlands Village—was situated between Walton and Weybridge in Surrey and had been built by Henry VIII as a hunting lodge. It was used as a palace until destroyed in the time of Cromwell. Each of the courtyards had formal gardens but outside the wall were the main gardens, orchards and parks.

By this time Tradescant had a son, John, old enough to help him. John had been educated at King's School, Canterbury, which he entered in October 1619 at the age of eleven, and left in 1623 with 'a good knowledge of the classics and a sound training in Latin' which was to stand him in good stead for the rest of his horticultural life.

The Tradescant house at South Lambeth was a brick, lath and plaster dwelling with tall graceful windows and a tiled roof. The entrance from the street was along a drive flanked by lawns. John Evelyn visited it and proclaimed the view from the turret as very fine 'it being so near London and yet not discovering any house about the country'. It was known as Turret House.

To the south was open countryside with the hamlet of Brixton nestling nearby. East was deer forest and in the north was Lambeth Palace. To the west lay the Thames. The grounds of the house extended to over four acres.

The Tradescant garden became famous and the house was soon being referred to as 'The Ark' because a room in it had been set aside as a museum to display all the strange things Tradescant had collected. These were continually being augmented by curios brought to the house by sailors and merchants returning from abroad. Both the Ark and the garden proved so attractive that visitors came flocking to Lambeth.

E

In 1637 Tradescant was offered the post of Keeper of the Oxford Botanical Garden but did not accept the appointment. He died the following year while his son was in Virginia collecting more plants—a task he had now taken over from his father. When John came home, he was appointed successor to his father as gardener to Charles I and held this position until the king's death, when he retired to Lambeth to work on the garden and museum. There he drew up an elaborate catalogue illustrated by the celebrated Wenceslaus Hollar, of the plants and shrubs growing in the Lambeth garden.

The list of fruit shows that the number of varieties of most plants had increased considerably. With apples, for example, there was a far wider range than had existed at the time of Parkinson and Richard Harris. They included :

Doctor Barchams	Quince	Great Russeting
Pome de Rambure	Summer Permaine	Summer Beiliboon
Master Williams	Winter Pearemaine	Puffing Pippin
Yellow Russeting	Gillefloure	Pome de Chastana
Harry	Violet	Pome de Renet
Ribon	Darling	Pome de Carpendu
Pome Mater	Stoken	Pome de Caluele
Russet Pippin	Pidg'ions Bill	Yellow Spising
French Pippin	The Kings	Dari Gentles
Dutch Pearmaine	M. Molins	Livinges
Black	Grey Costard	Mother Pippin
Barfolde Queninges	Winter Belliboorne	Russet Peare
Smelling Costard	Snouting	Keelings
John	Blandrille	Ginitings
Red Master Williams	Torne Crab	Black Pipin

The old pearmain, costard, quoining (queninges), pippin, and Reinette (Renet) are all represented here. Pome Mater is probably a mis-spelling of Pome water and the John is the Apple-John. Ginitings is almost certainly Juneating. But there is an impressive addition of new named varieties.

With pears, there was an even larger number of new names, though the Bergamot, Windsor and Bon Chrétein are still mentioned.

Binfeild	Winter Boon Critain	Hony
Gergonell	Summer Boon Critain	Mid-summer
Sir Nathaniel	Arundell	Winter Burgamot

Bacons Great Peare	Pallas	Poyer de Poydre
Rose Water	Hedera De Besa	Double floure
Poyer Messer Ian	Michaelmas	Sugar
Nutmeg	M. Motts	Bloud
Bishops	Paynted	Poyer Fran Rial
Orange Burgamott	Sliper	Winter Winsor
May	Greene Rowling	Summer Winsor
Greenefield	Swise	Poyer Irish Madam
Dego	Summer Burgamot	Poyer Dangobet
Scarlet		Poyer de Valet
French Popering		Poyer de Sauoyse
Snow		

There were also others with vague names such as 'greet 16 ounce', 'grete winter', and a 'french peare called R. Collanit'. Plums were also in wide variety and included :

Morocco, Spanish, Red peascod, Plum Dine, Damaske violet, Verdoch, Friers, Bowle, Nutmeg, White Rath, Peake, Apricocke, Orenge, Michaelmas damaske, Red Mirabolane, Monsiers, Perdigon, Kings, Queenes, Blacke, pruneola, Diapre Plum of Malta, Imperiall, Date, Musle, Damascene, Irish, Red plumordin Plume, Amber, Turke, Denny, Grene Oysterly, Grene mother, Frier, Sheffell Bulis, Impryall, Gante, Grene peascod, Damson and Pruon.

The cherry list showed the egriot (agriot) mentioned by Busoni and two, the Luke Ward and the Naples, mentioned by Gerard in his *Herball*. Of these two Gerard says :

the Luke Warde's cherrie is so called because he was the first that brought the same out of Italy : another we have called the Naples's cherrie, because it was first brought into these parts from Naples : the fruit is verie great, sharpe pointed, somewhat like a man's heart in shape, of a pleasant taste, and of a deepe blackish colour when it is ripe.

Gerard also mentions the Spanish cherry—another on Tradescant's list. But Tradescant also had the Swertes, Selinars, Cluster, Great Hart, Arch-Dukes, Tradescant's Double flower, Corone, Great Bearing, Chamelion, White and May.

Of apricots, there were the Barbarie (two sorts), Small Holland, Masculine, Long muske, ordinary and 'The apricocike that is both long and great'. Of nectarines, Roman Red, Sir Edward Sillard's Red, the little yellow, Bastard Red and white. Peaches included Tradescant's double flowered, Queens, White, Nutmeg, Peach de Troas, Newington, Carnation, Spanish, Devine, Roman, and Mallycotone.

A few vines were also to be found; parsley-leaved, Fronteneac, potbake, reison, currans, blue, and the 'buxtet grape which is very seildum rip'.

A few of the flowers (which the younger Tradescant was responsible for introducing from Virginia) were the originals of the herbaceous phlox, perennial lupin, michaelmas daisy, golden rod, dogwood, doronicum, evening primrose, passion flower, honeysuckle, and aquilegia.

The Tradescant museum housed a mixture of birds, animals, fish, insects, minerals, 'outlandish fruits', paintings, 'warlike instruments', garments, household utensils, coins and medals. Here, one could find :

Easter egges of the Patriarch of *Jerusalem*.

Aracari of Brazil, his beak four inches long, almost two thick, like a Turkes sword.

The claw of the bird Rock; who, as authors report, is able to trusse an elephant.

Dodar from the Island of *Mauritius*—it is not able to fly being so big.

Squeede from the basse in *Scotland*.

The bustard as big as a turkey, usually taken by greyhounds on *Newmarket-heath*.

Cloven and hairy-tongued lizards.

Figures and stories neatly carved upon plum-stones, apricock-stones, cherry-stones, peach-stones etc.

Flea chains of silver and gold with 300 links a piece and yet but an inch long.

A booke of Mr Tradescant's choicest flowers and plants exquisitely limned in vellum, by *Mr Alex Marshall*.

A piece of stone of Saint *John Baptists* tombe.

A brazen-ball to warme the nunnes hands.

Blood that rained in the *Isle of Wight*.

Henry the 8—his stirrupps, hawkes-hoods, gloves.

Edward the Confessor's knit gloves.

Anne Bullens night vayle embroidered with silver.

Exotic fruits such as the banana, mango and pineapple and capsicum were also included.

John Tradescant the Younger died in 1662 and 'The Ark' and its contents passed to an antiquarian called Elias Ashmole. He, in turn, left it to Oxford University where it became the Ashmolean Museum.

Once 'The Ark' had been moved from Lambeth, Turret House and gardens began to be forgotten. Two hundred years later the garden was totally neglected and the house empty and ruined. A few plants and trees were still growing among the weeds.

The tomb of the Tradescants at St Mary's Lambeth was repaired by public subscription in 1773 and an epitaph added:

> Know, stranger, e'er thou pass, beneath this stone
> Lie John Tradescant, grandsire, father, son . . .
> These famous antiquarians that had been
> Both gardeners to the rose and lily Queen,
> Transplanted now themselves, sleep here; and when
> Angels shall with their trumpets waken men,
> And fire shall purge the world, these hence shall rise
> And change their gardens for a Paradise.

A Tradescant stained glass window (paid for by American gardening societies) was put in the Ashmolean Museum, and the London Gardens Society later offered a Tradescant Cup each year for the best-kept police garden.

In Lambeth today, Tradescant Road and Walberswick Street run through the site of the old garden. In Meopham, Kent, where the elder Tradescant once lived by the village green, there is now a Tradescant Drive and a Lilac Avenue.

If this is not enough, the name will live on as long as the tender 'Wandering Jew' *(T. fluminensis)* and that hardy little herbaceous plant, the spiderwort *(T. virginiana)*, retain the name of Tradescantia.

CHAPTER SIX

SARAH SEWELL OF
COVENT GARDEN

MARKETS of one kind or other have been a feature of large towns since very early times. But always there seems to have been a check on where these markets could be set up and how they should be conducted. The Anglo-Saxon laws confined market business to cities and towns, and William the Conqueror later laid down that sales should take place only in cities, boroughs, walled towns, castles and other safe places. The City of London had been a market town for as far back as records go but, by the mid-seventeenth century, more and more people were taking up residence outside the city boundaries and needed to be supplied with food. When the Covent Garden area was laid out in 1630, many wealthy people went to live there and it soon became the custom for a few market gardeners and country folk to bring produce to this square several times a week for sale. Within 100 years it was a regular, thriving, market place.

One August morning in 1712 Sarah Sewell was at her stand in Covent Garden market awaiting a consignment of melons that Mr Cuffe, a market gardener at Nine Elms, was sending her to sell. The melons came by boat down the Thames and were no doubt landed at Strand wharves and then carried on the heads of porters all the way uphill to the market square.

In 1712, Covent Garden market was a small affair compared with what it was to become later. Sarah Sewell may have rented one of the sheds that had been erected along Tavistock Row, or she may have carried on her business in the open. At this period the market had been officially in existence for forty-two years, though selling of produce had gone on in the square for some years before that.

The first reference to a market in the churchwarden's accounts for St Paul's church, Covent Garden (designed by Inigo Jones) appears in 1656 when thirty shillings were paid out for 'painting the benches and seates in the market-place.' In the 1660s the Earl of Bedford decided that the market was worth developing and applied for the necessary royal charter. Such charters were not easily obtained since the right of holding markets was a prerogative of the Crown, though it could be transferred as a franchise to a subject.

The early markets were controlled by a court of Pye-Poudre ('dusty-foot') and this court was established in every fair or market by whoever owned or had the toll of the market. Under Pye-Poudre, people had to be tried and the punishment administered during the day or duration of the fair or market. Under common law, a rival charter market could not be set up within six and two-third miles of another charter market. Yet despite the fact that Covent Garden was considerably less than this distance from markets already in the City, the Earl of Bedford duly received his charter from Charles II in 1670. It gave him the right to hold a market for fruit, vegetables and other produce in a place

commonly called the Piazza near the Church of *St Paul Covent Garden* . . . within the rails there as without, every day in the week throughout the year, except Sundays, and the Feast of the Nativity of Our Lord, for the buying and selling of all manner of fruit, flowers, roots, and herbs, whatsoever, and upon these days for ever; together with all liberties and free customs, tolls, stallage, pickage, and all other profits, advantages, and emoluments whatsoever, to such market any way belonging, appertaining, arising, or coming, or with the same used, held or enjoyed. . . .

Though the earl was granted the charter in 1670, he did nothing much about it for eight years, during which the market business in the square, or 'piazza', increased considerably. The earl must then have decided to hand over the running of the market to someone else, as an arrangement was made with Adam Pigott and Thomas Day whereby, in return for a payment of £80 a year to the earl, they were given the right to erect and let buildings on the market site. This arrangement continued for twenty-one years, until the entire Bedford House estate was sold for building.

The best description of the Covent Garden area at the time of Sarah Sewell comes from Strype's edition of Stow's *Survey of London*. Strype, who wrote in 1720, describes it as :

a curious, large and airy square enclosed by rails between which rails and the houses runs a fair street. The square is always kept well gravelled for the accommodation of the people to walk there and is raised with an easy ascent to the middle so that the rain soon draineth off and the gravelly bottom becomes dry, fit to walk on.

In the middle of this garden within the rails 'is a stone pillar or column, raised on a pedestal, ascended by steps on which is placed a curious Sun-dial four square; having above it a mound gilt with gold, all neatly wrought in freestone.

On the north and east sides are rows of very good and large houses called the Piazzas, sustained by stone pillars, to support the buildings, under which are walks, broad and convenient, paved with freestone. The fourth side lieth open to Bedford Garden, where there is a small grotto of trees, most pleasant in the summer season; and on this side there is kept a market for fruits, herbs, roots and flowers every Tuesday, Thursday and Saturday.

It was on this Bedford Garden side that Sarah Sewell probably had her stand, though she may have been one of those who encroached upon the square itself. This gradual encroachment of the market was not received kindly by the inhabitants of Covent Garden, most of whom paid high rents to live in the modern houses. Another minute from the vestry of St Paul's contains a memorial addressed to the owner of the market :

The Market contrary to originall usuage has for many years abounded with divers ranges sheds shops and stalls many of which have been erected since the commencement of the present lease wherein several trades or occupations of sundry sorts are carried on and exercised and w[ch] your Memorialists conceive could never have been intended by your Grace to be permitted in an Herb-markett such as Covent Garden Markett originally was vizt. bakers, haberdashers, cookshops, retailers of Geneva and other spirituous liquors, and sundry other trades to the great annoyance and prejudice of severall tradesmen of the said Parish who pay large rents and great taxes for their houses.

The great number of stands wch have been erected for these seven years last past, as well in the High streets without the rails of the Square, as within, have not only been a very great inconvenience to the Parishioners but also the right and liberty of free passage from one street to another, round the Markett, has been thereby totally obstructed and taken away.

The memorial then mentions the stench and offensive smoke and concludes by hoping that the square will be restored to its 'pristine flourishing state'.

But nothing was done and the square, which was supposed to have been kept clear for the benefit of everyone, was more and more encroached upon by the market people. The column in the centre of the square took on the character of a market cross.

But when the market people had gone home there was still plenty of room for sport and amusements. John Gay in his *Trivia* of 1716 writes:

> Where Covent Garden's famous temple stands,
> That boasts the work of Jones' immortal hands,
> Columns with plain magnificence appear,
> And graceful porches lead along the square;
> Here oft my course I bend, when lo ! from far
> I spy the furies of the foot-ball war :
> The 'prentice quits his shop to join the crew,
> Increasing crowds the flying game pursue,
> O whither shall I run? the throng draws nigh :
> The ball now skims the street, now soars on high :
> The dexterous glazier strong returns the bound,
> And jingling sashes on the pent-house sound.

Puppet shows were always welcome, and Samuel Pepys records in his *Diary* for 1662, 'my wife and I to the puppet play in Covent Garden'.

For Sarah Sewell there was always the possibility of seeing someone in the pillory or being whipped at the tail-end of a cart. At late as 1730, one Mary Williams was whipped 'at a cart's tail thrice round Covent Garden market . . . for stealing oranges out of Mrs Vernon's greenhouse at Twickenham'. On Sunday mornings a bird market was held and sparrows, linnets, daws and magpies were sold. And if Sarah Sewell felt peckish, there was hot barley broth, rice milk and rice porridge to be bought from the women who sat around the base of the column. Into the square, too, came itinerant showmen.

But by Sarah Sewell's time, Covent Garden market was no longer a place just for the casual selling of produce. It had become quite big business and Sarah Sewell is the first stallholder to be mentioned by name. Richard Steele, in *The Spectator* of 11 August 1712, tells how during a boat journey down the Thames from Richmond he fell in with a 'Fleet of Gardiners bound for the several Market-Ports of *London*'. He goes on:

> It was very easie to observe by their Sailing and the Countenances of the ruddy Virgins who were Supercargos, the Parts of the town to which they were bound. There was an Air with the Purveyors for *Covent-Garden*, who frequently converse with Morning Rakes, very unlike the seemly Sobriety of those bound for *Stocks-Market*.
>
> I landed with Ten Sail of Apricock Boats, at *Strand Bridge*, after having put in at Nine Elmes and taken in Melons consigned by Mr *Cuffe* of that place to Sarah Sewell and Company at their Stall in *Covent Garden*.

At this period Covent Garden was rapidly replacing Stocks market in the City as the chief fruit and vegetable market, and other markets in competition with it included the small one on the southern end of London Bridge, previously mentioned, which, some time during the eighteenth century, was transferred to Rochester Yard where it became the Borough market, and Spitalfields on the opposite side of London.

In the City, besides Stocks market, there was Leadenhall, which had been started for poultry as early as 1309 but, by the eighteenth century, had built up quite a good business in fruit and vegetables. At Newgate in the first half of the same century, butchers had most of the space but, according to a petition to the Lord Mayor in 1720, much of its space was taken by 'gardiners, fruiterers, carts and pannyers all the morning of the market days so that there is hardly room to stir'.

The last attempt to establish a large fruit and vegetable market in the City proper was at Dowgate. A pamphlet published about the middle of the eighteenth century and entitled *Reasons for Fixing an Herb-Market at Dowgate* put forward the argument that Dowgate was much better situated than Spitalfields and Covent Garden to handle the produce which arrived over London Bridge. London Bridge at this period was important as the one over which Kent and Surrey market gardeners brought their produce by road, but when Westminster Bridge was built there was no longer any case for a market at Dowgate.

Hungerford was set up in 1678 to compete with Covent Garden. It was on the site of present day Charing Cross (BR) Station and was approached by a narrow entrance known as Market Street, between Craven Street and Charles Street on the south side of the Strand. It was named after its builder, Sir Edward Hungerford, a spendthrift who built the market in the hope of recouping his fortunes. The market was set up on the site of his home, Hungerford House, which he had pulled down. Hungerford market had a colonnade of shops leading down to the river and a landing stage, known as Hungerford Stairs, where the market produce was landed when it came by water. The market was particularly aimed at the market gardeners of the famous Neat Houses of Chelsea, a little further up the river. In 1685, Hungerford market became the property of Sir Stephen Fox, but it never succeeded in taking much trade away from Covent Garden.

Heavy produce for Covent Garden came in large quantities by water and most of it was landed at the Strand wharves near the Fox-under-the-Hill inn, whereas Billingsgate was the chief river port for landing vegetables for the City markets, and also handled large quantities of Kentish cherries.

From Queenhithe, there were regular sailings up the river as far as Maidenhead, Windsor, Chertsey and Kingston. On the outward journey, the boats carried manure and street-sweepings for the market gardens. The dung was usually first employed in forcing salad crops or for raising seedlings in hot beds and afterwards dug into the soil. Dung Wharf, next to Puddle Dock, was a depot for street refuse. Coming down river, the boats brought fruit and vegetables for the London markets.

The market gardens at this period and up to the coming of the railways were mostly within about fifteen miles of central London. Fruit was grown further away because it could stand the long, slow journey and the same applied to potatoes which were grown in Bedfordshire and even further afield. The majority of market gardeners, however, were still on the long level fertile stretches of land alongside the Thames, especially between London Bridge and Greenwich and up river around Fulham, Battersea, Chelsea, Putney and Brentford.

Apart from water transport, the two-wheeled cart drawn by horses was most used and the four-wheeled wagon was beginning to be seen. The horses could get lost in Covent Garden, as the following newspaper cutting bears out :

> Strayed from the Cart yesterday in Covent Garden, a Horse, broken winded, lame in the off Foot, brown before, mustled about the Mouth, and a brand Mark on the near Thigh behind, with the knob'd Shoes on and spare Harness, the Bridle marked with I and C. Half guinea reward.

For nearer and lighter carrying to market, women were used, particularly by market gardens near London during the strawberry season. This fruit was frequently carried in baskets on the heads of mainly Welsh, Shropshire and Irish women, who used to come to areas such as Fulham for the season. Round about midnight, these women would leave the market gardens each carrying about 40 lb of fruit and make their way in groups of up to a hundred to London. The easy carriage of these women was ideal for the safe transport of this delicate fruit.

It was probably one of these women whom Gay wrote about in his *Trivia*, though the time was autumn and the load then was apples.

> Doll everyday had walk'd these treacherous roads,
> Her neck grew warpt beneath autumnal loads
> Of various fruit; she now a basket bore;
> That head alas ! shall basket bear no more.
> Her booth she frequent past, in quest of gain
> And boys with pleasure heard her shrilling strain
> Ah, Doll ! all mortals must resign their breath,
> And industry itself submit to death :
> The cracking crystal yields; she sinks, she dies
> Her head chopt off from her lost shoulders flies;
> *Pippins* she cry'd; but death her voice confounds;
> And *pip, pip, pip* along the ice resounds.

It was not possible to travel alone on the roads because of footpads, and market gardeners as well as the strawberry women joined together for night journeys to the London markets. A Middlesex newspaper reported that :

> several Gardeners coming to Covent Garden were robbed by three footpads, armed each of them with a Brace of Pistols, on Walham Green, near Fulham, who took from one of the Gardeners near Eight Pounds, and from the others, what Money they had, after which they made off over the Fields to Hammersmith.

Women, in fact, did a great deal of the work in Covent Garden in the early days. In the eighteenth century, the Irish basket women of the market were notorious and no doubt Sarah Sewell employed them to carry goods bought from her. This was their official job, but they were capable of almost anything, as the following newspaper cutting of around 1730 bears out :

> Thursday evening an Irish basket woman of Covent Garden market was backed at odds to carry a *great fat man* in a basket, upon her head, to the Elephant and Castle, in the London-road, in the short space of 25 minutes. The *massive load of flesh* being properly placed the woman started off at quick time, followed by a concourse of persons, until she arrived at Waterloo Bridge, where, according to agreement, she was to receive a shilling. Here some altercation took place by the toll-keeper demanding ld for passage of *gentleman in the basket*. This weighty matter being speedily settled by paying, the *fair one* proceeded with her burden till she arrived at the toll-gate, at the Coburg Theatre, when the unwieldly gentleman exhibited some uneasiness by thrusting his legs out and the bets were made against the performance. The woman, however, threatening with an oath to throw him into a ditch if he did not keep quiet, proceeded and arrived at the Elephant and Castle a few minutes within the given time and received several presents from the crowd assembled.

Almost as notorious as the basket women were the flower and fruit girls. Their market language was earthy but out on the job of selling they had a number of quite pleasant cries. Street cries, of course, had long been a feature of London life and as early as the middle of the fifteenth century John Lydgate, a Benedictine monk of Bury St Edmunds, had written :

Then unto London I dyd me hye
Of all the land it beareth the pryse :
Hot pescodes, one began to cry,
Strabery rype, and cherryes in the ryse.
One bad me come nere and by some spyce
Peper and safforne they gan me bede,
But for lack of money I myght not spede.

Cherries 'in the ryse' were cherries still growing on the twigs, a favourite way of selling them for many years.

Well-known cries were :

Hot baked wardens—Hott !
Ripe speregas
Buy my four ropes of hard onyons
Delicate cowcumbers to pickle
Harrti choks
Whyt carots whyt
Round and sound, fivepence a pound, Duke cherries !
Fresh gathered peas, young Hastings !
Two bundles a penny, primroses, two bundles a penny.
Strawberrys, scarlet strawberrys !

Sometimes the cries were longer :

With mutton we nice turnips eat
Beef and mutton never cloy
Cabbage come up with summer meat
With winter nice savoy.

And longer still, though it is doubtful if this was ever sung :

Here's fine rosemary, sage and thyme
Come buy my ground ivy
Here's fetherfew, gilliflowers, and rue
Come buy my knotted marjorum ho !
Come buy my mint, my fine green mint
Here's lavender for your cloaths
Here's parsley and winter savory,
And heartsease which all do choose
Here's balm and hissop and cinquefoil
All fine herbs, it is well known.
    Let none despise the merry merry wives
    Of famous London Town.

Here's pennyroyal and marygolds,
Come buy my nettle-tops

> Here's watercresses and scurvy grass
> Come buy my sage of virtue, ho !
> Come buy my wormwood and mugwort
> Here's all fine herbs of every sort
> And southernwood that's very good
> Dandelion and horseleek
> Here's dragon's tongue and horehound.
>   Let none despise the merry merry wives
>   Of famous London town.

The scurvy grass was a kind of cress which got its name for its use against scurvy. It could be made into scurvy ale and as such was sold in the taverns. Another herbal drink was saloop, made of sassafras (a kind of bark) and the plants of the cuckoo flower genus. It was recommended for hangovers, and was particularly appropriate to the Covent Garden of the eighteenth century which had become notorious for its night life.

The simplers or herb gatherers supplied the herb shops in Covent Garden. From hedges and streams they collected watercress, dandelions, nettles, bittersweet, red valerian, feverfew, hedge mustard and many others.

The containers used by the early market gardeners were almost all made of wicker, willow being available in large quantities on the margins of streams and drainage areas in the gardening districts. The banks and islets on the Thames became famous for their willows : at one time there were basket-makers' huts along the banks of the Thames all the way from Staines to Fulham. Chiswick Eyot was a big centre.

The pottle was a tapered container used mainly for strawberries and held about half a pound of fruit. The pottles were packed into a large marne and it was the marne that the strawberry women carried on their heads to the London markets. The loade was a large, round basket which tapered towards the bottom and was fitted with a lid and handles. The barge was a four-foot long rectangular basket. The strike held 12 lb of fruit, while the pad was a small rectangular basket with a hinged lid used for peaches and other delicate fruit. The carts and vans were built to take a convenient number of containers.

Sarah Sewell must have seen many a strange sight in the early hours of morning as she made her way to her stand. Though market business was increasing in the daytime, Covent Garden was then best known for its night life. Many of the fine old houses had been taken over and turned into drinking dens, gambling houses and brothels, while bagnios, or Turkish baths, were particularly well patronised. Not surprisingly, Covent Garden was one of Hogarth's favourite resorts and several of his famous paintings depict scenes there. One, called *Morning*, shows the church and in front of it, the notorious Tom King's coffee house. In another, *Rake's Progress*, the night scene is reputed to have taken place in the Rose Tavern in Russell Street.

Certainly Covent Garden was no place to wander about in alone after dark. Apart from prostitutes, pimps and drunks, it was a gathering place for criminals and other delinquents. The watchmen, known as the 'Watch' or 'Charleys' did their best to keep order, but often it was a poor best.

The arrival of the market gardeners and other stall-holders in the early hours of the morning must have coincided with the lingering departure of many a habitué of the night, and it was the market that was to win in the long run.

William Forsyth.

James Lee.

Loading up in a Middlesex market garden in 1895.

Getting the produce to market early during the nineteenth century.

CHAPTER SEVEN

JAMES LEE OF HAMMERSMITH

AS cultivation of fruit and vegetables to feed the population of Britain increased, so there developed side by side with it an industry devoted to raising the plants the market gardeners needed on their holdings. Though not all the nursery trade dealt with this section of the horticultural industry, much business was done with the general public who were becoming increasingly interested in their own private gardens. The nurserymen not only provided the plants and gave advice on how to look after them but laid out and planted up both gardens and orchards. Most of the big nurseries were near the large towns to begin with, so that their customers were able personally to choose the plants they required. Most nurserymen prided themselves on having something new and different to offer each year, and many plant nurseries were set up by gardeners on savings accumulated during long years of service.

In the early part of the eighteenth century, while Sarah Sewell was busy selling produce at Covent Garden market, James Lee was born somewhere in southern Scotland, possibly in Selkirkshire.

The district must have been a very poor one for until 1725 there was not even one cart in Selkirk. There could have been little gardening and not much agriculture apart from the rearing of a few cattle, sheep and horses. Linen weaving was one of the chief occupations, and it is known that weavers were fond of growing flowers as a hobby. If, therefore, James Lee's parents were weavers, as they quite possibly were, they may have given him his love of flowers—a love which was to remain with him all his life.

Lee left home in 1732 taking with him 'a fine Toledo blade marked with the name of Andrea Farrara'—which gives us some idea of the perils a young man had to face in the eighteenth century. We have no idea whether he was called on to use this sword but we do know that he contracted smallpox at Lichfield, recovered and continued his journey to London, where he is believed to have gone to the house of the Duke of Argyll who owned Whitton Place, near Twickenham, and was famous for his love of trees and his collection of exotic plants. The garden at Whitton Place had been enclosed from Hounslow Heath and was surrounded on three sides by heathland and on the fourth by a plant nursery in which the duke raised his own trees and shrubs. Possibly, though there is no confirmation, Lee may have gone first to the Apothecaries' Garden at Chelsea, where the famous Philip Miller was in charge. If he did, it would probably account for his intimate knowledge of botanical terms. But if Lee worked under Miller, he must have left by 1736, for in that year the great Swedish botanist, Carolus Linnaeus, visited Miller, whereas in later life Lee said he had never met Linnaeus though he had a great deal of correspondence with him. Of course, it could have been that he was away from the Chelsea Garden at the time of Linnaeus' visit, or perhaps Miller did not bother to introduce Linnaeus to one who at the time could only have been a junior employee. Yet Lee was later to be the first to introduce Linnaeus' new system of botannical nomenclature into England.

Lee may also have worked at Syon House before going to Whitton. Gardeners of those days tended to move from place to place to gain experience. If he was at Syon, it would have been at the time when it belonged to the Dukes of Somerset and before it became the home of the Dukes of Northumberland.

Whatever happened to Lee, we do know that about 1745 he became a partner with one Lewis Kennedy in a nursery in Hammersmith known as The Vineyard.

Lewis Kennedy was six years younger than Lee and little is known about his early life except that he may have worked at one time at Chiswick, possibly for Lord Burlington. By the time he met Lee, he had already set up on his own as a nurseryman and no doubt Lee's connections and knowledge of botany influenced him in deciding upon the partnership.

At the time The Vineyard was established the trade for plants, and shrubs in particular, was becoming a vast one. Many large nurseries were setting up around London to cope with the demand. The large ones not only supplied the markets direct but also individual market gardeners. They also kept open house for the general public who were becoming more and more interested in gardening. Many of the nurserymen advertised their goods in catalogues in which the plants, shrubs and trees were arranged according to the latest botanical classification, which tended to be rather lengthy until the binomial system of Linnaeus was introduced.

In 1730, five years after Lee and Kennedy had started at Hammersmith, a *Catalogus Plantarum*—'a Catalogue of Trees, Shrubs etc for sale in the Gardens near London'—was published by a group of nurserymen who had their gardens around Kensington, Chelsea, Battersea, Hoxton, Putney, Fulham, Lambeth and Hyde Park Corner.

Men like Lee and Kennedy and others who advertised in the Catalogue were the cream of the profession. But not all nurserymen were of their standard. Thomas Fairchild a nurseryman at Hoxton writing in *The City Gardener* in 1722 says:

. . . Most of the People who sell the Trees and Plants in *Stocks* and other Markets are Fruiterers who understand no more of gardening that a Gardener does the making up of Compound Medicines of an Apothecary. They often tell us the plants will prosper, when there is no Reason or Hopes for their growing at all; for I and others have seen Plants which were to be sold in the Markets, that were as uncertain of growth as a Piece of Noah's Ark would be if we had it here to plant.

This was not something new. The Gardeners' Company had been formed over a hundred years earlier to deal with this situation and in theory at least, they had the power to seize sub-standard goods in the markets. But the Gardeners' Company was only for gardeners 'inhabiting within the City of London and within six miles compass thereof' though a move was made (but failed) to extend their influence over the whole of England and Wales and to incorporate 10 garden designers, 150 noblemen's gardeners, 400 gentlemen's gardeners, 100 nurserymen, 150 florists, 20 botanists and 200 market gardeners—which gives some idea of how the industry had grown.

However, there could have been little complaint about the quality of the goods supplied by The Vineyard nursery, which stood on the present site of Olympia—that is between Addison Bridge and Blythe Road on the north side of Hammersmith Road. Before Lee and Kennedy turned the land into a nursery it had been a vineyard—one of several in the Hammersmith district where the once flourishing industry of grape growing was to linger on into the nineteenth century. In 1778, James Gessop, gardener to John James of Hammersmith, 'made a quantity of exceedingly good wine from English grapes'. Vines also grew in the garden of the workhouse at Hammersmith and a resolution of the Select Vestry in 1825 laid down that the grapes belonged to the parish and should be sold on its behalf. At one time, there were several 'Vine Cottages' in the Hammersmith district, and old records talk of a 'vynehouse' in 1628 and of a wine-cooper in 1686. H. M. Todd in his *Vine Growing in England* says that a considerable amount of 'Burgundy' wine was once produced in Hammersmith.

When Lee and Kennedy set up their nursery there was a thatched cottage on their land, with wine cellars, which had evidently been used as a place from which to sell the wine. It could have been the 'vynehouse' mentioned above.

The Vineyard nursery was conveniently situated on the main road to London. It started in a small way but, as it attained success, so it grew until eventually it had many heated and cold glasshouses to produce the tender plants which had become so popular. A foreman to Lee and Kennedy at one period was J. Cushing who, in 1811, produced a book *The Exotic Gardener*. The full title was:

THE EXOTIC GARDENER in which the management of the hot-house, green-house, and conservatory, is fully and clearly delineated, according to modern practice: with an appendix containing observations on the soils suitable to tender exotics together with a table shewing the particular soil proper for each genus and a Calendarium Florum, for every month in the year: containing all the species known to be cultivated in the above departments.

In his introduction, Cushing says :

Such is the force of natural habit throughout the universe, that even vegetables, natives of the warmer climes, between or near the tropics, cannot exist when transported to the more Northern latitudes, unless art steps forward to their assistance; thence necessarily proceed the numerous glass erections throughout our Islands under the denominations of Hot and Green-houses, etc etc.

He goes on to say that a hot-house is :

a department, solely appropriated to the reception of those plants indiscriminately, which for the greater part of the Year require the aid of artificial heat to preserve, or bring them to a certain degree of perfection in our Northern regions. . . .

The book shows that glasshouses of one kind or other had already become quite common. Stoves were used in many of the new glasshouses, though Cushing's book does not deal with these. But Philip Miller, in the 1759 edition of his *Dictionary*, mentions 'dry stoves' which had heated pipes either in the floor or at the back of the house, and 'bark stoves' which had a large pit running almost the length of the house and which was filled with 'fresh Tanner's Bark' which generated the heat. Into this bed of bark the tender exotic plants were placed.

In 1760, James Lee caused a small sensation in the horticultural world with the publication of his *An Introduction to Botany containing an explanation of the theory of that science and an interpretation of its technical terms extracted from the works of Dr Linnaeus and calculated to assist such as may be desirous of studying that Author's method and improvements.*

Lee had been putting his knowledge of Latin to good use and his book was largely a translation of Linnaeus' *Philosophia Botanica*. Lee describes himself as a nurseryman and, in the preface, has this to say about his own part in the translating :

. . . He is far from desiring the World should conceive from the Appearance of his Name in the Title Page, that he is of sufficient Strength to undertake a work of this kind without Assistance. Though it had always been a Pleasure to him to study the Theory of his Profession, as far as the Business of it would allow leisure for, he is very sensible of his own Inability

to put the Materials of such a Work into a Form correct
enough to come under the Eye of the Public, and, were he
permitted, would readily acknowledge the Obligations he has
to those who have kindly helped him in this Undertaking, but
as some Injunctions oblige him to be silent on this Head, he
must content himself with having said this much to clear himself of any Imputation of Presumption or Arrogance.

No-one knows exactly who the helpers referred to were, or why
they wanted to remain anonymous. Perhaps they were not so
convinced of the value of the Linnaeus system as was Lee.

Up to the time of Linnaeus (or Carl von Linné as he afterwards became) plants were given names which amounted to a
short Latin description. Rhubarb, for example, was *Hippolo-
pathum maximum rotundifolium exoticum*. These long names
sufficed in the days when the total number of plants was small
and introductions were rare. For his system, Linnaeus grouped
together those plants that he found to have flowers of similar
construction. The most important groups or units were called the
genera and within the genus came a division into *species*. For
these two units, Linnaeus evolved his new method of nomenclature, using merely a generic and a specific name. (The method
has been extended since to include sub-species, cultivars etc.) To
take the example of rhubarb again, it now became *Rheum
rhaponticum, Rheum* being an old name for medicinal rhubarb
and *rhaponticum* meaning the Black Sea area.

Lee's *Introduction to Botany* was long regarded as a standard
work and its publication made him famous and brought visitors
from all over the world to The Vineyard. The second edition contains a dedication to Linnaeus.

The permitting me to dedicate the following sheets to you, is
the highest Point of my Ambition, and a Mark of my Gratitude
and Esteem, for the Instruction and Pleasure I have received
in the perusal of your truly learned and excellent Works. . . .
The *Introduction to Botany* owes its first Principles to you,
being collected from your Works, particularly the *Philosophia
Botanica*, nothing of it can be called mine, but its being
cloathed in an English Dress; the addressing you in Front of
my Book can therefore add nothing to your Instruction or
Fame; your giving me Liberty to prefix your Name there does
me the greatest Honour, at the same time that it tells the World

this Dedication is free from Interest and Flattery, as it is to you whom I have never seen, nor ever expect to see; my only Motive in this proceeds from a grateful sense of your superior merit, and to applaud you for the useful Lesson you have given to Mankind.

Although the *Introduction to Botany* was Lee's greatest work he also published in 1787, a pamphlet, *Rules for Collecting and Preserving Seeds from Botany Bay*, and the list of botanical terms in his botany book was later published separately as *Termini botanici*.

Lee was also the probable author of the catalogue of The Vineyard published in 1774. This seventy-six page book is divided into :

Hardy trees and shrubs; herbaceous plants; greenhouse plants; plants for a dry stove or glass house; stove plants; fruits; kitchen garden seeds; seeds of evergreen and deciduous trees and shrubs; annual, perennial and biennial flowers; farm seeds; garden tools.

Though The Vineyard carried this wide range of plants, it specialized in exotics, and it has been estimated that they introduced some 135 plants into England during the life-time of James Lee. These plants came from North America, Siberia, South Africa, Chile, Madeira, China, Australia, Mexico, Guinea, Sierra Leone, West Indies, as well as from most of the countries of Europe. All sorts of people sent plants and seed to the nursery. From Russia, came rare seeds sent by Peter Simon Pallas, Councillor of State to the Emperor of all the Russias, who was an eminent naturalist and traveller. J. Pringle of Madeira sent plants and bulbs from Madeira and ixias and gladioli from South Africa. Colonel Peterson, in command of a company of soldiers sent to protect the convicts at Botany Bay, found time to collect plants. Joseph Banks also brought seeds from Botany Bay. Australian (New Holland) plants were a feature of The Vineyard, which was also celebrated for its roses.

But if there is one plant with which The Vineyard can be identified it is the fuchsia. They did not introduce it to England but they were the first to put it on sale. Several versions of how they managed to get a stock of it exist, but the following account

given in the *Lincoln Herald* for 4 November 1831 is easily the
most amusing, if perhaps not the most truthful :

> Old Mr Lee, a nurseryman and gardener near London, well-
> known fifty or sixty years ago, was one day showing his
> variegated treasures to a friend, who suddenly turned to him
> and declared, 'Well, you have not in your collection a prettier
> flower than I saw this morning at Wapping.' 'No! and pray
> what is this phoenix like?' 'Why, the plant was elegant, and
> the flowers hung 'in rows like tassels from the pendant branches,
> their colour the richest crimson, in the centre a fold of deep
> purple . . .', and so forth. Particular directions being demanded
> and given, Mr Lee posted off to the place, where he saw and
> at once perceived that the plant was new in this part of the
> world. He saw and admired. Entering the house, 'My good
> woman, this is a nice plant. I should like to buy it.' 'Ah, sir,
> I could not sell it for no money, for it was brought me by my
> husband, who has now left again and I must keep it for his
> sake.' 'But I must have it.' 'No, sir!' 'Here,' (emptying his
> pockets) 'here is gold, silver and copper.' His stock was some-
> thing more than eight guineas. 'Well-a-day, but this is a power
> of money, sure and sure.' ' 'Tis yours, and the plant is mine and
> my good dame shall have one of the first young ones I rear to
> keep for your husband's sake.' 'Alack, alack!' 'You shall, I
> say.' A coach was called in which was safely deposited our florist
> and his seemingly dear purchase. His first work was to pull off
> and utterly destroy every vestige of blossom and blossom-bud,
> it was divided into cuttings which were forced into bark beds
> and hot beds, were re-divided and sub-divided. Every effort
> was used to multiply the plant. By the commencement of the
> next flowering season Mr Lee was the delighted possessor of
> three hundred fuchsia plants all giving promise of blossom. The
> two which opened first were removed to his show house. A lady
> came. 'Why Mr Lee, my dear Mr Lee, where did you get this
> charming flower?' 'Hem! 'tis a new thing, my lady—pretty!
> 'tis lovely.' 'Its price?' 'A guinea; thank your ladyship.' And
> one of the two plants stood proudly in her ladyship's boudoir.
> 'My dear Charlotte! where did you get . . . etc.' 'Oh! 'tis a new
> thing I saw at old Mr Lee's. Pretty, is it not?' 'Pretty! 'tis
> beautiful! Its price?' 'A guinea; there is another left.' The
> visitor's horses smoked off to the suburb; a third flowering plant
> stood on the spot where the first had been taken. The second
> guinea was paid and the second chosen fuchsia adorned the
> drawing room of her second ladyship. The scene was repeated
> as newcomers saw and were attracted by the beauty of the

plant. New chariots flew to the gates of old Lee's nursery grounds. Two fuchsias, young, graceful and bursting into healthy flower were constantly seen on the same spot in his repository. He neglected not to gladden the faithful sailor's wife by the promised gift, but ere the flower season closed three hundred golden guineas clinked in his purse, the produce of a single shrub of the widow in Wapping, the reward of the taste, decision, skill and perseverance of old Mr Lee.

Even allowing for some journalistic licence on the part of the *Lincoln Herald*, it does seem that James Lee was an astute business man.

This particular fuchsia is believed to have been *Fuchsia coccinea*, a native of Chile, which had reached Kew Gardens the year before, in 1788.

Another popular introduction was *Buddleia globosa* with its little orange balls of flowers. Many heaths and pelargoniums (geraniums) were also introduced.

The Vineyard nursery by this time was famous and many illustrious visitors came to it. One who stayed with the Lee family for a while was Pierre-Joseph Redouté, who later was to become artist to the Empress Josephine and to produce wonderful paintings of many of the flowers grown at La Malmaison.

Sir Joseph Banks, though twenty-eight years younger than Lee, must have visited the nursery from time to time. Banks' botanical interest began while he was still at school and throughout his life he was very active in the horticultural world, travelling to Newfoundland and Iceland to collect plants and sailing round the world with Captain Cook. He founded Kew as a botanical garden and helped to start both the Linnean Society and the Royal Horticultural Society. He was president of the R.H.S. for forty-two years and his scientific collection and library eventually went to the British Museum.

Lee's partner, Lewis Kennedy, died in 1783 and his son, John Kennedy (born 1759), became Lee's partner. John Kennedy was an able botanist and was responsible for the description of plants in Henry Andrew's *Botanist's Repository* and Page's *Prodromus*. John Kennedy married twice and had twenty-one children. He was adviser to the Empress Josephine and helped plan and stock her garden at La Malmaison. The genus *Ken-*

nedia is named after him. In 1818, John sold out his share in The Vineyard and retired to Eltham in Kent, where he died in 1842.

James Lee had one son and three daughters. When he died in 1824, his son James took over the nursery and ran it so efficiently that the famous horticultural writer, J. C. Loudon, described it as 'unquestionably the first nursery in Britain or rather the world'. He added much new land, going as far afield as Bedfont and Hounslow, and brought in many novelties from abroad, including azaleas from Russia and chrysanthemums from China.

Sir Walter Scott visited the nursery in 1828 and noted in his *Journal* :

> . . . drove to Lee and Kennedy's and commissioned seeds and flowers for about £10, including some specimens of the Corsica and other pines. Their collection is very splendid, but wants, I think, the neatness that I would have had expected in the first nursery garden in or near London. The essentials were admirably cared for.

As the years went by, all the land was sold. In 1855 some went for the railway but The Vineyard acquired fresh land in Ealing, Isleworth and Feltham in lieu. Then, in 1885, came the building of West Kensington Gardens and the first of Olympia's halls, and the last entry for The Vineyard nursery in the Hammersmith rate books is dated 1894.

CHAPTER EIGHT

WILLIAM FORSYTH OF ST JAMES'S

FOR the early horticulturist, the prevention of pests and diseases was just as important as it is today, though very different methods were used as there was little knowledge of chemicals. The emphasis was on good cultivation to produce healthy plants which could, to some extent, withstand the attacks of many pests and diseases. But there is no reason to think that the quality of the final produce was then any higher, or in fact as high, as it is today. Almost certainly, on the whole, it was lower. Apart from good cultivation, infected plants were often pulled up and burned as soon as any sign of infection was noticed. With large trees, it was the custom to cut out any infected part—a 'remedy' that could often prove fatal to the tree. Washes of various kinds were used to get rid of such things as mildew and 'blight'. From time to time, someone would come up with an idea for curing one or other of the common complaints and, such was the need, they always aroused interest whether they were of any value or not.

One who was to play a prominent part as one of the earliest professional 'tree doctors' was William Forsyth, a Scotsman who at one time worked under Philip Miller at the Apothecaries' Garden in Chelsea.

William Forsyth was born 'somewhere in Aberdeenshire' in 1737. Little is known of his early days except that he was believed to have been at one time at Syon House in Middlesex. He must have been at the Apothecaries' Garden when he was about thirty-four or so because when Miller retired in 1771 it was he who took over his job. At once he began reorganising the garden, sometimes to the dismay of his associates, especially when he cut down many of the old trees. But he added considerably to the collection of plants and built one of the earliest rock-gardens from stones from the Tower of London and lava brought from Iceland by Sir Joseph Banks.

In 1784, at the age of forty-seven, Forsyth was appointed gardener to King George III at Kensington and St James's and thus became one of the foremost horticulturists in the land. Yet towards the end of his career (when he was sixty-three), Forsyth became involved in a horticultural 'scandal' that certainly did not help his reputation.

In 1799 England was at war with France and oak was in much demand for ship building. But much of the oak, especially in the royal forests, was found to be diseased and the Commissioners of the Land Revenue Office asked Forsyth for advice. They came to him because he had a wide selection of fruit and other trees under his care at Kensington Gardens and was known to be very interested in ways of preventing disease and decay in old trees.

At Kensington, Forsyth had found a good deal of canker in the apple trees and plenty of gumming in the plums and cherries. His remedy was to cut out as many diseased branches as he dared and, in the case of large and badly infected trees, to head them right back. To help the wounds heal he used a concoction of his own devising.

When the Commissioners approached him with their problem he boasted that he could cure most infected trees and render even seriously diseased trees 'fit for the Navy as though they had never been injured'. He also informed them that the remedy was known only to himself 'as it is not a secret drawn from books or learned from men, but the effect of close application and repeated experiments.' He hinted, however, that this information could be put at the Government's disposal for a suitable fee.

The Commissioners came to see Forsyth at Kensington and left impressed by what he showed them. In fact, they were so impressed that they presented a petition to the king:

> . . . to give directions for making such enquiries as shall be
> thought necessary for the purpose of ascertaining the efficacy
> of a remedy invented by William Forsyth, for curing defects
> in trees, arising from injuries in the bark; and in case the same
> shall appear likely to be of public utility, to order such recom-

pense to be made to the said William Forsyth on the disclosure thereof, as his Majesty shall judge proper; and to assure his Majesty, that this House will make good the same.

A committee of twelve, consisting of members from both Houses of Parliament, was appointed, with instructions to pay particular attention to the effect of Forsyth's special preparation on forest trees, especially the oak.

The committee went to Kensington Gardens and took a close look at the many trees Forsyth had treated, examining both the fruit trees and the forest trees. The committee included the Marquis of Abercorn, Lord Frederick Campbell, Sir George Yonge, John Rolle, Philip Stephens, C. M. Pierrepont, William Pulteney, Robert Barclay, Hans Sloane and William Mainwaring and they duly reported: 'we have every reason to believe . . . that Mr Forsyth's Composition is a discovery which may be highly beneficial both to individuals and the public.' On receiving this report the Treasury recommended that Forsyth should be given £1,500 at once and another £1,500 after an extended trial of the special preparation.

On the receipt of the first £1,500 Forsyth published his recipe. Its full title was:

Directions for making a composition for curing diseases, defects and injuries, in all kinds of fruit and forest trees, and the method of preparing the trees and laying on the composition.

These directions were:

Take one bushel of fresh cow dung, half a bushel of lime rubbish of old buildings (that from the ceilings of rooms is preferable), half a bushel of wood ashes, and a sixteenth part of a bushel of pit or river sand: the three last articles are to be sifted fine before they are mixed; then work them well together with a spade, and afterwards with a wooden beater, until the stuff is very smooth, like fine plaster used for the ceilings of rooms.

Instructions for its use followed:

. . . cutting away all the dead, decayed, and injured part, till you come to the fresh, sound wood, leaving the surface of the wood very smooth, and rounding off the edges of the bark with a draw-knife or other instrument, perfectly smooth, which must be particularly attended to; then lay on the plaster about one-eighth of an inch thick, all over the part where the wood or bark has been so cut away, finishing off the edges as thin as possible : then take a quantity of dry powder of wood ashes mixed with a sixth part of the same quantity of the ashes of burnt bones; put it into a tin box, with holes in the top, and shake the powder on the surface of the plaster, till the whole is covered with it, letting it remain for half an hour, to absorb the moisture; then apply more powder, rubbing it on gently with the hand, and repeating the application of the powder till the whole plaster becomes a dry smooth surface.

This was all that needed to be done. Forsyth then stated on oath that this was :

> . . . a true account of the method of making and using the Composition . . . for curing diseases, defects, and injuries, in fruit and forest trees; . . . which Composition was applied by him to the trees in His Majesty's Gardens at Kensington, shewn to the noblemen and gentlemen to whom it was referred to examine the efficacy of the said Composition.

Not content with this, Forsyth followed up with a small book entitled *Observations on the Diseases, Defects and Injuries in all Kinds of Fruit and Forest Trees*. This gave the same information but enlarged on it. It also added a suggestion for improving the composition 'by mixing it up with a sufficient quantity of urine and soapsuds and laid on with a painter's brush'.

Possibly not much more would have been heard of the so-called cure had not Forsyth decided to write a full-scale book on fruit-growing. He was encouraged in this by another Scotsman, James Anderson, who edited a monthly magazine *Recreations in Agriculture*. Anderson published in his magazine a long article on Forsyth's discoveries and claimed that he had persuaded Forsyth to write a full-scale book.

The book came out in 1802. It was 372 pages long with the title :

> *A Treatise on the Culture and Management of Fruit-trees; in which a new method of pruning and training is fully described, to which is added a new and imported edition of 'Observations on the Diseases etc' with an account of a particular method of*

cure, published by Order of Government by William Forsyth, gardener to His Majesty at Kensington and St James's, member of the Oeconomical Society at St Petersburg, etc etc . . . London, Printed by Nicols and Son, Red-Lion Passage, Fleet-Street for T. N. Longman and O. Rees, Paternoster-row; T. Cadell, Jun., W. Davies, Strand; and J. Debrett, Piccadilly.

Though full particulars of the cure now became available to all, few had the knowledge or the time to challenge it. One man however had both—a Herefordshire squire, Thomas Andrew Knight, who was a keen and knowledgeable horticultural scientist. Knight had become well known a few years previously through the publication of his *Treatise on the Culture of the Apple and Pear*, and in the second edition of this little book he added a criticism of Forsyth's 'plaister', as he chose to call it, saying 'I do not place much confidence on any topical application to the wounds or diseases of vegetables.'

When Forsyth elaborated on his cure in his new book, Knight replied with a pamphlet suggesting that Anderson had written Forsyth's book for him with a view to sharing the profits. He then related how he (Knight) had gone incognito to see Forsyth, pretending to know nothing about fruit. He had been shown, he said, trees which had been cut back and treated with the 'plaister' and Forsyth had told him that the treated branches which had sprouted again were only three years old. Knight himself put them at five. He added that Forsyth seemed astonished that his visitor did not show more surprise at the work.

Knight's view, put simply, was that a piece of old dying tree could never produce a vigorous and healthy young tree. 'Is a little lime, cow-dung and wood-ashes,' he asked, 'capable of rendering immortal that which the great God of nature evidently intended to die?' In any case, said Knight, this 'plaister' was nothing new. A wash composed of lime, cow-dung and wood-ashes had been used in Herefordshire almost half a century before. 'But,' he added sarcastically, 'it's wonderful effects were not then known!'

Asked how he accounted for all the old, rotten plums and cherry trees at Kensington which Forsyth had restored to health,

Knight replied that he had not seen them nor could he do so
because the thing was impossible.

> And as to the enormous crops of fruit which I must have
> seen . . . I really cannot speak, the plaistered trees having
> almost wholly failed to bear any in the only season that I was
> in Mr Forsyth's garden.

He added :

> It will, however, probably not be difficult to bring evidence of
> some kind that His Majesty's table was always abundantly
> supplied with fruit, even the year when I was at Kensington;
> and as the distance from Kensington Garden to Covent
> Garden is not greater than to which fruit may be conveniently
> carried, I can readily believe it.

This implication that Forsyth was buying fruit at Covent
Garden market to supply what the gardens of Kensington failed
to provide stung Forsyth to a refutation in the second edition of
his book in 1803. Meanwhile, he had obtained important backers
for his work, among them the Oeconomical Society of St Petersburg, whose secretary wrote to Forsyth as follows :

> His Excellency Count Anhalt solicits me to express, in your
> own language, the pleasure which the communication of your
> useful discovery has given him, and the learned body over
> whom he so worthily presides. The Count has already taken
> the necessary steps, by desire of the Society, to have your little
> dissertation translated and printed in the Russian language, in
> order to diffuse the advantage it holds out, as widely as possible,
> over this vast Empire.

Another supporter was Thomas Davis, author of *The Agricultural
Survey of Wiltshire*, who wrote :

> I was happy in having an opportunity the other day in shew-
> ing the effects of your plaster . . . to *Lord Spencer,* who was
> both pleased and astonished with it. You may at any time refer
> to me for proofs if you want them.

Yet another whom Forsyth brought to his support was the
Portuguese ambassador to the United Kingdom, the Chevalier
d'Almeida who, on returning to Portugal, had sent for Forsyth's
book to learn how to deal with diseased orange trees. Forsyth
had sent him instructions and a 'cask of the composition'.

Thomas Andrew Knight.

Thomas Rochford.

Joseph Rochford.

The Royal Exotic Nursery at South Kensington in the Victorian era.

But Knight still attacked:

> I assert that new and old wood, whenever cut, broken or decayed, never did unite in any one instance in any English tree; that a wound in the wood of such a tree never was healed, though it becomes covered by the annual layers of succeeding years. . . .

And again:

> I further assert that Mr Forsyth never filled up any tree, in which the old and new wood united with, or were not readily discoverable from, each other. You will perhaps tell me that the decision of the gentlemen deputed by the House of Commons disposes of my assertions.
>
> I have great respect for those gentlemen, but I would rather take their opinions on some other subjects than on the growth and formation of timber; and the acquirement of a parliamentary reward by Mr Forsyth affords a much better proof that he was paid for an important discovery than that he made one.

Despite the controversy, or maybe because of it, Forsyth's *Treatise* sold well and the first edition of 1,500 copies was cleared within a year. In the third edition, published in 1803, he took the opportunity to publish a letter carrying the names of eight eminent medical men, including that of J. C. Lettsom, a famous London physician, Fellow of the Royal Society and a keen amateur gardener. The letter, addressed to Forsyth, read:

> As you had the goodness lately to give us an opportunity of examining several trees in Kensington Gardens, in various stages of renovation, or filling-up with new wood; and as reports have been circulated, tending to discredit the efficacy of your process; we feel it is an act of justice, not only to you, but to the Country, which is deeply interested in your discoveries, thus publicly to declare that the statements you have published on the subject contain nothing more than the truth.

On reading this, Knight went into action again. He wrote to Lettsom and offered 200 guineas if he or his friends could produce a single foot of timber restored 'after being injured to the state asserted by Mr Forsyth'. Next, he offered 100 guineas if Lettsom could show a transverse section of a tree substantiating Forsyth's claim to be able to restore hollow trees, and a further

100 guineas for a transverse section of a tree in which old and new wood were incorporated. Yet another 100 guineas was offered if Lettsom could produce a piece of oak or elm which, after being cut, broken or decayed, had 'formed a heart or incorporation to the width of a single inch, in the manner asserted'. As arbitrator, Knight proposed the President of the Royal Society.

Lettsom refused on the grounds that, as a practising Quaker, he could not gamble, nor did he take up the challenge in any other way.

While all this was going on, Forsyth died, but the dispute continued for another year, mainly in the pages of the *Gentleman's Magazine* and among the leading gardeners and scientists of the day. Lettsom eventually accepted a proposal to exhibit specimens at a meeting of the Horticultural Society, but did nothing about it. Knight was invited to go to Kensington and see for himself again but declined, saying it was useless :

> . . . I have no doubt but that you will be able to produce abundant verbal evidence that trees which were once all rotted away, except a part of the bark, are now perfectly fit for all Naval purposes; and as His Majesty's trees cannot be cut down and internally examined, such evidence can only be set aside by the common sense of the country. I am the less anxious to attend, because all my friends in town (and among them I have the honour to reckon some of the best judges of vegetation in Europe) assured me that scarcely any person believed Mr Forsyth's assertions, or paid the least attention to your attestation.

Lettsom's reply to this was to publish two pictures of Forsyth's transverse sections of restored trees, whereupon Knight pointed out that anyone with the slightest knowledge of timber could see that one of the pictures clearly showed a wound which was over thirty years old and so must have been healed before Forsyth had even come to live at Kensington. As for the other picture, it showed no evidence of union of new and old wood.

Forsyth may or may not have been deliberately pulling a fast one on the public, the Navy and the government, but as a gardener he was no charlatan and his *Treatise on the Culture and Management of Fruit Trees* was a best-seller for many years. As well as giving instruction on how to grow the various types of fruit, it contains many indications of how things were in the horticultural industry at the beginning of the nineteenth century. Cherries, he says at one point, are :

a very considerable article of traffic in the London markets and in the markets of most towns throughout the kingdom, employing a great number of people during the summer season in gathering, carrying to market and selling them. . . .

He strongly advises growing a few for, as well as being ornamental, they can, he says, be profitable and :

gentlemen of small fortune, who are at a great expence with their gardens and plantations, may in a great measure reimburse themselves by selling their cherries and other fruit (for which there will be plenty of chapmen) and thus enjoy at an easy rate the pleasures of a rational and useful recreation.

In all parts of the country, he goes on, there are persons employed in collecting fruit for the markets 'and to hawk it about from place to place'. Surely, he says, it is better to sell it to them than to let it rot on the ground, or be devoured by birds and insects. He quotes a gentleman near Kensington Gardens who had thirty-nine Morello cherry trees along a 176-yard wall and who sold his fruit to a market gardener for 3s per lb and made himself between £30 and £40 a year 'besides supplying his own family'.

He gives long lists of recommended fruit. The best apples for eating raw, he says, are :

Acklam's Russet, Cawood Timely, Chardin's Sans-pareil, Early Nonpareil, Golden Pearmain, Hubbard's Pearmain, Large Golden Pippin, Oxhead Pearmain, Pomphilia and White Pippin.

For a succession of pears, he gives :

Summer: Musk, Green Chissel, Jargonelle, Summer Bergamot, Summer Bonchrêtien
Autumn: Orange Bergamot, Autumn Bergamot, Gansel's Bergamot, Brown Beaurré, Doyenné, Swan's Egg.
Winter: Crasane, Chaumontelle, St Germain, Colmar, D'Auch, L'Eschasserie, Winter Bonchrêtien, Bergamot de Pasque.

With gooseberries, he mentions ten varieties as being common :

Green Gascoin, Smooth Green, Early Black, Small Early Red, Large Smooth Dutch Yellow, Hairy and Smooth Red, Large

Smooth Yellow, Large Rough Yellow, Common, and Large White, Champaigne.

He gives a list of the 'largest new sorts (of gooseberries) shown in Lancashire last summer (1800) with their colour and weight, communicated by Messrs McNiven, Nurserymen, Manchester.' This was the era of gooseberry shows in the north of England and the list shows the amazing range of colour and weight and the fascinating names given to most of the show varieties:

Red Gooseberries

	dw	gr		dw	gr
Alcock's King	16	15	Withington's Scepter	13	7
Alcock's Duke of York	16	1	Brundit's Atlas	17	1
Boardman's Royal Oak	15	4	Dien's Glory of England	16	2
Chapman's Peerless	15	21	Fisher's Conqueror	17	19
Fairlow's Lord Hood	14	5	Hall's Porcupine	13	20
Fox's Jolly Smoker	15	8	Worthington's Glory of		
Lomax's Victory	16	11	Eccles	14	10
Taylor's Volunteer	16	17	Mason's Hercules	13	16
Robinson's Crudus	13	7			

Yellow Gooseberries

	dw	gr		dw	gr
Brundit's Sir Sidney	15	22	Davenport's Creeping		
Hamnet's Kilton	15	9	Ceres	16	0
Hill's Golden Gourd	13	17	Leigh's Prince of Orange	15	0
Hill's Royal Sovereign	17	10	Parkinson's Goldfinder	14	5
Davenport's Defender	15	12			

Green Gooseberries

	dw	gr		dw	gr
Blakeley's Chissel	17	0	Boardman's Green Oak	14	1
Brundrit's Tickle Toby	14	6	Chadwick's Hero	13	10
Dean's Lord Hood	15	10	Mill's Langley Green	16	2
Read's Satisfaction	15	4	Robinson's Stump	13	21
Smith's Green Mask	13	20	Yates's Duke of Bedford	14	11

White Gooseberries

	dw	gr		dw	gr
Adams's Snow Ball	12	22	Woodward's White		
Chapman's Highland			Smith	17	2
White	12	0	Atkinson's White Hall	14	8
Gibson's Apollo	14	20	Davenport's Lady	15	0
Kenyon's White Noble	13	6	Holding's White Muslin	13	0
			Moor's White Bear	14	19

His book also deals with various pests and diseases. His favourite remedy is urine and lime-water mixed and used as a wash. He recommends this for mildew, unless things are very bad when he suggests:

> Take tobacco one pound, sulphur two pounds, unflaked lime one peck, and about a pound of elder-buds; pour on the above 'ingredients ten gallons of boiling water; cover it close, and let it stand till cold; then add as much cold water as will fill an hogshead. It should stand two or three days to settle : then take off the scum, and it is fit for use.

Aphis, he says, should be destroyed as soon as possible. For this:

> Take some fine wood ashes mixed with one third part of fine unslaked lime, and throw it on with a common dredging-box, till you have covered the undersides of all the leaves where you find the insects : this should be done in the morning early while the dew is on the leaves, which will cause the powder to adhere to them; letting them remain so covered with the powdered lime for three or four days. Then mix unslaked lime and soft water, or water that has been exposed to the sun a week at least, at the rate of half a peck to thirty-two gallons, and stir it well two or three times a day for three or four days. . . . With this liquid, after the lime has subsided, give the trees a good watering . . . by a barrow engine . . . this should be repeated once a day for six days, which will destroy all the aphides.

For the engine, Forsyth recommends one designed by a Mr Winlaw which, he says, may be obtained from Messrs Chieslie & Yowle, 72 Margaret Street, Cavendish Square.

For red spider, he suggests plenty of moisture as a preventative including 'frequent watering . . . with limewater . . . throwing it plentiful in the undersides of the leaves'.

Caterpillars should be carefully picked off and the best method to prevent them getting on to the trees is 'to scrape the stems with a piece of bone or wood made in the form of a knife, taking care not to bruise the bark; and afterwards to wash the tree . . . with an equal quantity of soapsuds and urine mixed'.

He puts forward a plea for more observation of the ways of caterpillars:

It would be of great service to get acquainted as much as possible with the economy and natural history of all these insects, as we might thereby be enabled to find out the most certain method of destroying them. Were a few of each sort of caterpillars put in a box or case, and fed with leaves of such trees as they generally live upon, they might be observed from time to time until they came to the chrysalis, and from that to the moth or butterfly state, and thus a more perfect knowledge of them might be obtained.

Of birds he has little to say except that they can be a nuisance and that the best prevention is to cover the trees with nets or bunting, 'a sort of cloth of which ships' colours are made.' These nets, he says, will admit a free circulation of air to the fruit, and will soon dry after rain : they will also be a good covering for the trees in spring, in cold, wet, or snowy weather.

There were many men of Forsyth's calibre and standing among the horticulturists of the late eighteenth and early nineteenth centuries. Many, like him, were gardeners to famous people and many also wrote books on horticulture. But only Forsyth has gone down in history as the man who invented a 'plaister' to ensure good timber for the Navy. It has never been denied that he was a good horticulturist but, in the matter of the 'plaister', there are many who consider he must have been a fraud.

CHAPTER NINE

ANDREW KNIGHT OF LUDLOW

THROUGHOUT the early centuries, improvements in plants had been obtained mainly by selecting the best plants and retaining their seed. The method was slow though a 'sport' did occasionally appear which had beneficial characteristics and represented a real step forward. Other methods included vegetative propagation, such as the taking of cuttings or buds from selected plants, but there was no planned breeding of new plants until the mid-eighteenth century. Then, fired by the success of a Leicestershire farmer, Robert Bakewell, in improving the stock of sheep and cattle by applying scientific principles to their mating, a Herefordshire squire set about transferring pollen from one selected plant to another in order to produce new varieties of fruit and vegetables, some of which remain with us today.

None other than the man who had so vigorously challenged William Forsyth's claim to be able to cure dying trees, this Herefordshire squire—Thomas Andrew Knight—was the second son of a fairly well-to-do clergyman who had a private income from the family business of iron smelting around Madeley and Coalbrookdale in Shropshire. Born in 1759, he went to school at Ludlow and Chiswick before entering Balliol College, Oxford where, it was said, 'he managed to acquire as much Latin and Greek as most of his fellow students, though he spent less time about it, and much less than he devoted to field sports'. Six feet tall, with blue eyes and light brown hair, Knight, after Oxford, settled down to the life of a country gentleman at Elton Manor, near Ludlow.

As a boy at Wormesley Grange, near Hereford, he had learnt a great deal about fruit, for the Herefordshire orchards were famous. And when he married and settled at Elton, he turned his attention to many of the problems of fruit growing, especially where it concerned the making of cider and perry.

In the quietness of his Queen Anne house with its green lawns and small stream, its walled garden and surrounding orchards, he began his observations on apple canker, the debility of grafted trees and a host of other matters which can best be classified as vegetable physiology.

To begin with, Knight carried out most of his experiments just to please himself. But a chance meeting with Sir Joseph Banks, Secretary of the Board of Agriculture, changed this attitude. Banks persuaded him to make the results public and encouraged him to come to London from time to time to meet other scientists. It was through Banks that Knight was persuaded to read his first paper to the Royal Society. This was in 1795 when Knight was thirty-six.

Knight had an original line of thought in producing new plants. The fruit trees in Herefordshire were mainly increased by grafting. A few new seedlings had been found and propagated from time to time but, in general, the fruit orchards consisted of poor trees bearing small, rather insignificant apples and pears. Many of the old trees were slowly dying.

Knight formed the theory that any grafting which joined a piece of old tree with the root of a young tree only perpetuated the old tree and, as the old trees became older, so the grafting material taken from them became weaker. Therefore, Knight argued, it was essential to produce as many new varieties as possible from seed so that the resulting trees would be full of vigour. The parents of the new varieties had to be carefully selected and the pollen from one parent placed on the stigma of the other. From the resulting progeny, the best were selected and grown on.

Knight's first paper to the Royal Society dealt with this subject. It was entitled *The Inheritance of decay among fruit trees and the propagation of debility by grafting*. He followed up the paper with a small book *A Treatise on the Culture of the Apple and Pear etc.* which dealt more fully with the subject as well as touching on many other points. The apple, he wrote in the book, was not the natural product of any particular soil or climate but owed its existence to human art. The first varieties cultivated in England were imported from the Continent but nobody knew quite when. Many were introduced by a fruiterer of Henry VIII and others at various times afterwards. But by the seventeenth century, most of the varieties in common use were those which had been the latest to be introduced. He says :

> . . . no kind of apple now cultivated, appears to have existed more than two hundred years. . . . From the description Parkinson, who wrote in 1629, has given of the apples cultivated in his time, it is evident that those now known by the same names are different, and probably new varieties; and though many of those mentioned by Evelyn, who wrote between thirty and forty years later, still remain, they appear no longer to deserve the attention of the planter.

Of the apples mentioned by John Evelyn, Knight said that the Moil, Redstreak, Must and Golden Pippin were in the last stages of decay and the Stire and Foxwhelp almost as bad. The Teinton Squash pear, however, was thought to go back to the beginning of the sixteenth century at least. And another local variety, the Barland, was almost as old.

Much of Knight's book is taken up with observations on the manufacture of cider and perry which were being produced in large quantities in Herefordshire. At one point he warns his readers against false claims. Perhaps he had Forsyth and his 'plaister' in mind.

> I would wish to guard the inexperienced planter against trustin to the assertions of nursery-men, particularly in the neighbourhood of London; who will promise to send him trees of the Golden Pippin, or any other kind of apple, that will not canker. But they are much in the habit of promising what they cannot perform, and are extremely ignorant of every thing beyond the mere routine of their profession; and (as usually happens) positive in proportion as they are ignorant.

He also warns against the bringing in of pests on plant material, especially one particular pest that was troubling the London area :

> The insect, which has produced such destructive effects on the apple trees, round London, during the last ten years is said to

have lately become less abundant; but apple trees should on no account be taken from districts where this destructive insect exists into others where it is not known.

The idea of improving fruit by crossing was not a new one. Bacon (1561-1626) in one of his essays had written :

> . . . the compounding and mixture of plants is not found out, which, nevertheless, if it be possible, is more at command, than that of living creatures, whereof it were one of the most noble experiments touching plants to find this art; for so you may have a great variety of new plants and flowers yet unknown. Grafting doth it not : that mendeth the fruit, or doubleth the flower, but it hath not the power to make a new kind—for the scion overruleth the stock.

But it was left to Knight to put into serious practice the method of crossing chosen parents. The following are varieties raised by this method and which he considered worth preserving :

Apples: Grange Apple, Downton Pippin, Red Ingestrie, Yellow Ingestrie, Breinton Seedling, Bringewood Pippin, Yellow Siberian, Siberian Pippin, Foxley Apple, Siberian Harvey, Siberian Bittersweet, Spring-grove Codling, Herefordshire Gillyflower.
Cherries: Elton, Waterloo, Black Eagle.
Strawberries: Elton, Downton.
Plums: Ickworth Impératrice.
Nectarines: Impératrice, Ickworth, Downton, Althorp.
Pears: Monarch, Althorp Cressane, Rouse Level, Winter Cressane, Belmont.
Potatoes: Downton Yam.
Peas: The Knight.

There were also many other unnamed varieties including a large, long-keeping currant, a large purple plum, two damsons, several other potatoes and some cabbages.

In apples, Downton Pippin was a cross between Isle of Wight Orange Pippin and Golden Pippin and can still be found. It is a small round apple with a bright yellow skin and brown spots and at its best from November to January. Yellow Ingestrie is the only other variety recorded today. This apple gets its name from Ingestrie, the seat of Earl Talbot, though the original tree was at Wormsley Grange. There are said to be still a few left in

Kent orchards. It is a smallish yellow apple which matures in September.

The plum Ickworth Impératrice gets its name from Ickworth, near Bury St. Edmunds, and can still be found. It is a large, oblong purple plum much marked with yellow dots and splashes. The flesh is soft and juicy. Its season is October and it was formerly much used for drying, the practice being to leave the plums on the tree till they shrivelled and then dry them for use later in the year.

It is the cherry, however, which does most to perpetuate the memory of Knight today, though the names have become rather obscured and some tend to vary in different parts of the country. Waterloo is perhaps the best known as it is grown in all the main cherry districts of England and can also be found on the Continent and even as far afield as America. A dark red, almost black cherry, it has a wide reputation as a high-quality fruit and cherry connoisseurs will eat Waterloo in preference to all others. But Waterloo is becoming increasingly difficult to find, largely because it is unpopular with farmers in these days of high picking costs owing to its habit of hiding its scattered fruit instead of growing it in clusters. When Knight's cherry orchard (planted about 1808) was visited by British fruit experts in 1926, only seven trees remained. Two were identified as almost certainly Waterloo, one was thought to be Black Eagle and another Elton Heart. Scions of these trees were taken and grown on at East Malling Research Station near Maidstone, Kent.

Knight contributed to the *Transactions of the Royal Society* the results of numerous experiments on such subjects as the 'foundation of plants', 'rise of sap', and 'vessels through which sap ascends and descends'. The object he always had in mind was utility, and he had to be convinced of some practical application before he would start an investigation.

His work on roots is acknowledged to be one of his most important. In this, he put forward the hypothesis that, though roots and branches went in the direction they did because of the pull of gravity, certain other natural causes could act in opposition and divert the radicle as well as the fibrous roots. Knight used machinery devised by himself to demonstrate this. In his paper

On the direction of the radicle and germen during the vegetation of seeds read before the Royal Society on 9 January 1806, he described this machinery :

> Having a strong rill of water passing through my garden, I constructed a small wheel similar to those used for grinding corn. . . . Round the circumference of the latter numerous seeds of the garden bean were bound. The radicles of these seeds were made to point in every direction . . . the machinery, having been the workmanship of myself and my gardener, cannot be supposed to have moved with all the regularity it might have done, had it been made by a professional mechanic.

But, concluded Knight,

> I conceive myself to have fully proved that the radicles of germinating seeds are made to descend, and their germens to ascend, by some external cause, and not by any power inherent in vegetable life : and I see little reason to doubt that gravitation is the principal, if not the only agent employed in this case, by nature.

Another hypothesis he put forward was that ascending sap undergoes a change in its progress, something like that which takes place in the blood of animals in its passage through the lungs, and that later this sap descends through the bark, depositing in its course an inner layer of bark and a new layer of wood, while the old external bark cracks and peels off the branch or stem as the tree grows larger.

In 1806, Knight was awarded the Copley medal for his work on vegetable physiology, the first of a long list of awards he was to receive over the next twenty-five years. The full record is as follows :

1806	Royal Society Copley gold medal.
1814	Horticultural Society gold medal.
1815	Large silver medal for Black Eagle cherry.
1817	Large silver medal for Waterloo cherry.
1818	Large silver medal for Elton cherry.
1822	Banksian silver medal for new pears.
1836	New large gold medal.
1801	Society of Arts silver medal for turnip drill.
1815	Caledonian Horticultural Society gold medal, 'In testimony of their gratitude for his valuable discoveries,

the result of patient and laborious research in vegetable physiology—science having been his guide'.

1826 Massachusetts Agricultural Society medal (a circular plate of silver, two and a quarter inches in diameter, inscribed 'The Massachusetts Society for Promoting Agriculture, to Thomas Andrew Knight, Esq. of Downton Castle, England, as a tribute to an eminent physiologist, and a benefactor to the new world').

1830 Swedish Academy of Agriculture grand silver medal.

Apart from his horticultural work, Knight also became well known for his agricultural activities, which included the breeding of Herefordshire cattle. This breed had been improved considerably by Lord Scudamore, who had imported cattle from the Continent to cross with local breeds. When he died in 1671, Knight carried on the work of improving the breed. He became a founder member of the Herefordshire Agricultural Society in 1797 and, both at local shows and at Smithfield, his cattle obtained many prizes. In 1790, George III presented him with a Merino ram which had been brought into the country to help improve the wool of our native breeds. Knight crossed the Merino with the Ryeland and obtained a mixed breed. Another venture was to cross Norwegian ponies with London dray horses.

In 1803, through Sir Joseph Banks, Knight met Sir Humphrey Davy, one of the leading experimentalists of the day. Davy was about to deliver a course of lectures on the chemistry of agriculture to the Board of Agriculture and discussed several points with Knight before doing so. The acquaintanceship ripened into a warm friendship and a correspondence began which continued until the death of Sir Humphrey in 1829.

In 1804 Knight received a letter from Sir Joseph Banks which read:

It having occurred to some of us here, that a Horticultural Society might be formed, upon a principle not very dissimilar from that of the numerous Agricultural Societies, which, if they have done no other service, have certainly wakened a taste for agriculture, and guided the judgments of those who wished to encourage it; two meetings have been held in order to commence the establishment, the proceedings of which I enclose to you. You will see that I have taken the liberty of naming you as an original member.

The Horticultural Society (later the Royal Horticultural Society) was duly formed with the Earl of Dartmouth as president and John Wedgwood as secretary. The first part of the *Transactions* was published in 1807 and contained two papers by Knight, forerunners of many others it was later to receive from him. The Society obtained its charter in 1808 and in 1811, with Lord Dartmouth dead, Knight was elected president and held the office until the time of his death.

Knight and the secretary, Sabine, gave the Society new impetus and soon its supporters included not only men of science and practical gardeners but a large proportion of the aristocracy and wealthy people of the country. Information and new plants came from all over the world and were made equally available to members. In 1818, the Society established a small experimental garden at Kensington but this was found to be limited in scope and also too near the centre of London. So, thirty-two acres of garden were taken over at Chiswick and the stock removed there in 1822. Another innovation was the award of medals. The Society's first gold medal went to Knight 'for his various and important communications to the Society, not only of papers printed in the *Transactions* but of grafts and buds and his valuable new fruits.' A few years later the Banksian medals were introduced and when, in 1835, new designs for the medal were adopted the first impression of the large gold medal was presented to Knight for 'the signal services he has rendered to horticulture by his physiological researches.' Knight's reply, on being informed of this award, was characteristic of the man.

> I feel highly honoured and flattered by the wishes of the members of the Horticultural Society of London, that the first impression of their new gold medal should be presented to me, and I shall receive it with very great pleasure, provided I be permitted to subscribe a sum equivalent to the cost, to be employed in liquidation of the debt of the Society, but not upon any other conditions.

By the spring of 1809, Knight and his family had left Elton Hall, where he had lived since his marriage, and moved to Downton Castle which belonged to his brother, Richard Payne Knight. Here he took over the house and management of the estate while his brother lived in a small cottage in the grounds during the time he was not in London. At Downton, Knight continued his experiments and the several new varieties containing the word Downton were raised during this period. The name Elton had occurred in many of the earlier varieties.

At Downton, Knight divided his time between philosophical and horticultural investigations and the duties of a country gentleman. In 1827, his only son Andrew was accidentally killed and two years later his great friend, Sir Humphrey Davy, died. During the previous year Davy had published the fourth edition of his *Lectures on Agricultural Chemistry* which he had dedicated to Knight. On the eve of his departure for the Continent he had written to Knight :

> I have sent a copy of my Agricultural Chemistry to the Horticultural Society, addressed to you. If any thing it contains relating to Vegetable Physiology is of value, it is owing to you, and in my dedication I perform at once an act of public duty and of private friendship. Should I recover my health, I have various plans of scientific labour, principally on natural history : and in the wintery state of my mind, I live principally on hope. . . .

Sir Humphrey Davy died at Genoa without returning to England. In his will, he left Knight a seal ring bearing the impression of a fish in memory of days they had passed together on the banks of the Teme.

Knight was keen on many other field sports besides fishing. He spent a great deal of his time learning about animals and was very particular as to the way in which game and poultry were killed for the table, often superintending the operation himself so that he could be quite sure that as little cruelty as possible was practised. He himself ate little animal food.

An impression of Knight towards the end of his life is given by Sir George Stewart Mackenzie in the *Edinburgh Chronicle* of September 1838. He had been to visit Knight at Downton.

> The venerable and talented proprietor of Downton, surrounded by a princely domain of ten thousand acres of rich and beautiful country, thinks of nothing but of what may be useful to his fellow-creatures. He received us with that unostentatious but kindly welcome which displayed the true spirit of hospitality;

regarding a visit as a favour conferred on the host, and not on the guest; and which at once excites mutual benevolence, that operates like magic in giving birth to friendship. . . .

Our venerable host, active and energetic in his seventy-eighth year as a man of forty, is one of those rarities among men, that know everything—who can put their hand to everything, and give a sound philosophical reason for what they do. He is one who can discern rottenness in church and state, as well as canker in a fruit-tree, and can fathom both.

Knight felt strongly on many subjects. In politics, he was a Whig of the old school and was opposed to voting by ballot, extended suffrage and so on. His memory was very retentive and it is said that at the age of seventy-nine he learnt by heart the whole of Campbell's poem *The Last Man*.

In his youth, he had been considered delicate but for most of his life he enjoyed almost uninterrupted good health, apart from dyspepsia in his old age. In 1838, on his annual visit to London, he died suddenly. He was buried at Wormesley beside his brother and son.

Thomas Andrew Knight is regarded today as a pioneer of scientific methods as applied to horticulture. This country squire living quietly in the pleasant countryside between the Wye and the Teme acquired a reputation and left a memory that will not easily be forgotten among horticulturists.

At Croft Castle, near Hereford, which was once owned by the Knight family and now belongs to the National Trust, a small garden has been constructed where many of the trees, shrubs and plants introduced by Knight are still preserved.

Walnut time at the market at the beginning of the twentieth century.

Cabbage planting about 1900.

Horse transport from market garden in 1860.

CHAPTER TEN

THE ROCHFORDS OF TOTTENHAM

A CRUDE form of glasshouse is known to have been used by the Romans for producing out-of-season vegetables and fruit. It consisted of a pit covered with slabs of talc and was heated by hot air and decaying manure. The first glasshouse of which any record exists is one at Heidelberg, in Germany, which, in 1619, was used to protect orange trees from frost during the winter. The first glasshouse in England was probably at the Apothecaries' Garden in Chelsea in 1684. Development was slow but steady for the next 150 years until curvilinear glass was introduced, to be followed a little later by steam heating. Then came the repeal of the window tax and lower duties on timber, and within fifty years the commercial glasshouse industry was well established.

With London still expanding in the 1880s and the smoke nuisance always a serious problem, market gardeners and nurserymen around Tottenham to the north of London began to look for places less crowded and less contaminated in which to settle and build new and larger glasshouses.

The Lea Valley ('Lee' is possibly the more correct spelling, but common usage since the sixteenth century is in favour of 'Lea') on the northern fringe of London had at that time reasonably priced and fairly level land with a plentiful supply of water from shallow gravel or underlying chalk. It also had good roads and easy gradients—an important factor in days of horse traffic.

Soon the glasshouse nurseries of men such as Rochford, Larsen, Stevens, Shoults, Cobley, Pollard and Hamilton were familiar sights in the Lea Valley. The Rochfords were one of the first to go there.

Michael Rochford, who had left Ireland in 1840, was steward to Lord Feversham of Duncombe Park, Helmsley, Yorkshire. In

1857 he moved south to Tottenham and built a nursery at Page Green, not far from the banks of the River Lea, on what is now the site of the Tottenham Hotspur football ground. Here he grew pineapples and grapes for market and pot plants, particularly solanums, ficus, ferns and palms. Here he also raised six sons—all of whom became growers.

One son, Joseph, proved to be mechanically-minded and his father encouraged this by giving him a workshop in which the boy spent most of his evenings when he was not at home studying books on engineering, mechanics, chemistry, plant physiology and kindred subjects. In the workshop, he built among other things, a fifty-inch bicycle, a steam velocipede and a saw bench with varying speeds which he used mainly for making sash bars for glasshouses. Joseph was of small physique and short in stature but, according to a fellow grower writing many years later, 'head and shoulders above his contemporaries . . . combining maximum diligence and exceptional ability'.

In 1873, Joseph and his brother John persuaded their father to let them build some large new glasshouses and to do all the work themselves. At this period large glasshouses were still, comparatively, in their infancy, though sheet glass had been invented by a Birmingham firm in the 1830s. Joseph Paxton, the celebrated head gardener to the Duke of Devonshire, had paved the way in 1837 when he had put up a conservatory at Chatsworth which was 277 ft long and 123 ft wide, at that time the largest glass structure in the world.

In 1862, J. Sweet of Leyton, in Essex started erecting glasshouses using large panes of sheet glass which allowed extra light to reach the plants as well as being more economical.

Joseph and John Rochford may have seen these houses of Sweet's before they started building and it is possible that another firm, Beckwith, had already made a start with wide-paned glasshouses nearer home at Tottenham itself. C. W. Shaw in *The London Market Gardens*, published in 1879, describes some houses which must have been built several years previously :

> The houses in which growers for market cultivate their plants and flowers are generally span-roofed; light and airy, with a path running down the centre; as a rule little attention is paid

to painting and glazing in such places, what is done being performed when work is slack by men employed on the place.

He continues :

> The best examples of plant houses I have seen in market gardens are those belonging to Messrs Beckwith & Son, of Tottenham; they are span-roofed without rafters, the sashes in which the glass is fixed being of iron and placed at such distances apart as to admit a pane of glass 2 ft wide. By being thus constructed every possible ray of light is taken advantage of, and to this may be attributed in a great measure the almost marvellous results in the way of culture obtained there.

Another pioneer glasshouse builder was Duncan Tucker of Tottenham, who was to provide many of the glasshouses in the early Lea Valley days.

Shaw also gives an interesting account of one of the earliest heating systems for a commercial glasshouse :

> The heating apparatus consists of seven powerful horizontal tubular boilers each of which measures from 10 feet to 12 feet in length and 6 feet to 8 feet in width, and weighs nearly 9 tons. They were prepared from plans furnished by the proprietor and are found to be more economical, powerful and durable than those of more complicated construction. To these boilers are attached upwards of seven miles of 4-in piping, and in ordinarily mild seasons they consume 600 chaldrons (a chaldron was 35 bushels) of coke and 250 tons of coal, besides an enormous quantity of breese, small coal, cinders etc.

Sometime after 1873, the Rochford brothers designed the Rochford tubular boiler and always claimed that they were the first to make a horizontal tubular boiler. But did they get their idea from Beckwith or was it vice-versa? Certainly the Rochford boiler became famous in after years.

Another early glasshouse grower in the north of London was Peter Kay of Finchley. He started in 1874 and by 1899 had $18\frac{1}{2}$ acres of glass. In all, he had 161 glasshouses heated by twenty-five and a half miles of four-inch piping. One of the blocks consisted of twelve houses each 400 ft long, 36 ft wide and 15 to 18 ft high. A rainwater reservoir covered two acres and held 5,000,000 gallons, the water being pumped from the reservoir to a tower, from which it was piped to all parts of the nursery.

The output from this nursery in 1899 amounted to 100 tons of grapes, 100 tons of tomatoes and 20,000 dozen cucumbers.

The Rochfords remained in the forefront of the fast developing glasshouse industry. They were the first to glaze without top putty, relying on brads or paint to hold in the glass. They were the first to use Portland cement for pipe joints, and to them also goes the credit for introducing the raised tower or tank into which water was pumped to provide sufficient pressure to allow the watering by hose-pipe of plants in a glasshouse. This did away with the old hand-held watering can or self-propelled outfit and was a great labour saver. To the Rochfords also is given the credit for the familiar ventilator system using a lever outside the glasshouse to adjust the vents according to the weather conditions.

The glasshouses which the two brothers put up in 1873 suffered calamity in 1876 when a violent hailstorm broke most of the glass. There was no insurance against hail damage in those days though, a little later, growers did get together and form their own insurance company. Undeterred, the brothers took the opportunity to improve the houses still further in rebuilding, making the panes of glass even larger and replacing entire roofs.

Five years later Joseph Rochford married and asked to be allowed to have his own nursery. His father, judging the time was ripe for a move further still out of London, bought eight acres of land at Turnford, near Waltham Cross, in Hertfordshire. The land was on the lower terraces of the Lea Valley, where the brick earth and fine sandy loams were deep. Here, on 17 August 1882 Joseph Rochford set up on his own, there then being only one other grower in the area producing solely for the markets.

Cucumbers, grapes, flowers and ferns were the traditional crops of these pioneer glasshouse growers. These and pineapples had also been the main items produced by the Rochfords at Tottenham.

The pineapple had been a speciality of Michael Rochford's when he first came south from Yorkshire and he was probably one of the last in England to grow them as a market crop. With the improvement in transport, so many began to come from abroad that it soon became almost impossible to grow them at a profit in England. The few that were grown were arranged to ripen in late summer, when foreign competition was at its lowest. The most popular home-grown varieties were Queen and Black Jamaica.

Grapes were to keep going for many more years, but these, too, gradually succumbed to ever-increasing imports. In the early Lea Valley days, the main varieties were Black Hamburgh, Gros Colman, Madresfield Court and Muscat of Alexandria. The glasshouses to produce the earliest crops were planted with Black Hamburgh, Gros Colman, Black Alicante, Lady Downes and Muscat of Alexandria, all of which were expected to be ripe by the middle of May. Madresfield Court did not ripen until August but was highly appreciated on the markets because of its jet black colour and excellent flavour. It was a particular favourite in the high-class shops of Covent Garden's Central Avenue. By the mid-twentieth century, grapes were still being grown by the Rochfords, though by then they were one of the few firms growing them on a large scale. In 1956 they still had seven acres under glass. At Turnford, the only variety left by then in sufficient quantities to send to market was the Colmar, and these were grown mainly for the Christmas trade. A few were sent to market at the end of September and the season continued until the arrival of South African grapes at the end of January. With these established vines (some had been planted soon after Joseph had moved to Turnford in 1882), the heat in the houses was put on in January when a catch crop of lettuce went in and was out again before the vine laterals which would have shaded the crop had broken. The cultivation, which had probably changed little in seventy years was as follows :

About 17 or 18 laterals allowed to each rod and all surplus buds rubbed out. On a full crop about 25 bunches left to each rod. The best bunches selected and where possible only one bunch left on each lateral. During the growing season a temperature of around 66 deg F and in summer just about enough heat to keep the atmosphere dry. The vine rods trained along wires—one wire for the rod and another for the laterals. Watering was done during the growing season but not much while the grapes were ripening.

Thinning (a highly-skilled job, but a good worker could do

20 bunches an hour) gave shape to the bunch and correct spacing for the berries to swell.

Blood and potash as a feed during the growing season and after cropping forking over the ground and an application of base manure of bone meal, horn and potash. The soil thoroughly flooded. Vines pruned after the foliage had died down and the laternals being cut back to any eye at the base.

Cucumbers had been popular for many years and by 1878 one large nursery at Potter's Bar was sending 25,000 cucumbers a year to the London markets. They were grown in low span-roofed houses with three-foot beds on either side and in some cases a bed in the centre for melons. The main varieties of cucumbers grown for market at the end of the nineteenth century were Telegraph, Syon House, Sutton's Perfection and Rabley Prolific. Rochford's Market became popular a little later on. Cultivation was as follows :

> Seed sown in small pots which were plunged into beds of coco-nut fibre. When large enough the plants potted up into four-inch pots and afterwards planted out in the beds in the glasshouses. First sowing early December and first houses planted up a month later. Other.houses planted up in succession for cropping until September or October. Houses used for the early crop generally had pipe heating. Plants were trained up trellis fitted twelve inches from the glass, the main shoots being led upwards until their points were within one foot of the middle rafter directly over the pathway when they were stopped.

Ferns in their hey-day were sold both in pots and as fronds for mixing with cut flowers or for decoration on their own. During the Tottenham period, the fern most in demand was the maiden-hair, *Adiantum cuneatum*. Easy to grow and easy to look after, it was usually propagated by division of the root, though at times special varieties were increased by spores or seeds. When the plants were large enough, they were pricked out and potted on, until finally they were sold in five or six-inch pots, occasionally in larger ones.

Shaw mentions a Tottenham grower who grew maidenhair fern in twelve-inch pots :

> . . . and the fronds . . . far surpass any which I have seen in any other establishment near London. When these large speci-

mens become exhausted from constant cutting they are pulled
to pieces and potted into eight-inch pots. Each plant is expected
to furnish sufficient fronds during a year to bring in 15s—the
average price being 9d a bunch of about a dozen fronds.

Pteris ferns were also liked by the public because they grew
well in a small pot and lasted well both when in the pot and
when cut.

Palms, too, were much in demand. These were raised mostly
from imported seed sown in pots or pans and pricked out later,
potted up into six-inch pots and then hardened off before being
sent to market.

Around Christmas, solanums found a ready sale and most
market growers produced several varieties. The dwarf 'Weather-
ill's Hybrid' with a mass of large scarlet berries was a favourite.
Some growers planted the young solanums in the open and potted
them in the autumn, but the more successful method was to take
cuttings in the spring and immediately put them into a heated
house. When the berries began to swell, the plants were taken
out of doors to colour up.

The aspidistra made its name by its ability to thrive in the
same pot for a long time and to withstand dust and heat. It could
be obtained with green, yellow or white-striped leaves and was
propagated by cutting up the leaves.

Though the aspidistra is often thought to have been the
ubiquitous pot plant of the Victorian age, the plant that sold best
was the indiarubber plant, *Ficus elastica* : this flourished in the
same pot for years and stood up well to the smoky atmosphere
of London. It was propagated by taking the young tips of growing shoots and growing them on.

Other pot plants extensively grown were capsicum, myrtle,
verbena and coleus. Compact hardy shrubs such as euonymus,
yew and thuja were also a thriving business.

But the twentieth-century crop for the Lea Valley was to be
the tomato. Joseph Rochford quickly realised this and a large
proportion of his new Turnford nursery was given over to the
cultivation of this vegetable (or fruit, to be botanically correct).
Three-quarters of an acre of glass went up the first year and five
years later he had put up another ten houses, each 170 ft by 27 ft.

It is on record for this latter operation that the first brick was laid on the day before Good Friday and that by the Saturday before Whitsun (forty-four days) the houses were finished and a crop planted. Two crops of tomatoes a year were grown in the new houses, all in pots.

Even by the 1870s, the tomato was still known to many as the love apple and it was some time before the public accepted it as a salad vegetable. The first large supplies came from Italy where, in areas around Naples and Rome, tomatoes were grown on a very large scale and heavy supplies sent to Britain during the early summer. Picked green and packed in sawdust in large wooden cases, the tomatoes were allowed to ripen in transit. America sent canned tomatoes.

At first, the majority of tomatoes in Britain were outdoor-grown and these, during warm and favourable seasons, could prove quite profitable. Cultivation was as follows:

Seed sown in spring in frames on a hot-bed on which had been placed four or five inches of rich soil. Seed was slightly covered with soil. At three inches high plants were lifted and placed two to a six-inch pot and the pots plunged into a hot-bed. Towards mid May plants were hardened off and from the beginning of June plants for the earliest crops were planted out in favoured positions such as a fruit wall, warm border or spent mushroom ridge. The second batch of plants went into an open but warm place in rows three feet apart each way. Sometimes trenches were dug and filled with heating material to force the plants. If frost was expected inverted flower pots were put over the plants. Only the two strongest shoots were left to a plant and every alternate lateral removed as soon as it appeared. When several good clusters of fruit were set on the remaining shoots, the points were pinched out to induce increased bulk in the fruit. The ripest fruit was picked off twice a week but if there was a threat of frost the whole crop would be gathered and placed under glass to ripen.

For market, the tomatoes were packed in round sieve and half-sieve baskets, covered with rhubarb leaves and fastened down with hazel twigs. The fruit was sold by the sieve, half-sieve or dozen. During the main season, good tomatoes made around twopence to threepence a pound. Seven to twelve shillings a sieve was a good average price for September and October.

The English weather being what it is this outdoor growing was always tricky. So once the big new glasshouses were available, tomatoes were grown in them and so given a much longer season, while marketing was made more continuous and even. With the help of heat, tomatoes could be produced out of season and, having less competition from abroad, could be very profitable.

In 1883 Michael Rochford, the grower who came from Ireland, died, content perhaps that all his sons were in the industry and all making names for themselves. Later most of them moved to the Lea Valley. The elder son, Thomas, went to the Turnford area in 1888 and began to cultivate lily of the valley, tulips, ferns and many other kinds of pot plants, as well as the usual grapes, tomatoes and cucumbers. He was a pioneer in the retarding of plants and had a large refrigerator built to retard lily of the valley, *Azalea mollis*, *Lilium longiflorum* and other flowers. To begin with, this refrigerator was just a small non-conductive chamber fed with cold air from an oil engine but, as the years went by, it became larger and much more elaborate.

Flowers and pot plants were sold from Thomas Rochford's own stands in Covent Garden. Palms were introduced later and by 1914 thousands a year were being exported to the United States. At one time there were two acres of orchids and eight to ten million corms of lily of the valley being forced every year. Hydrangeas were another speciality and also nephrolepsis fern, of which *N. todeaodies* and *N. rochfordii* originated here. Thomas Rochford went on to build a business which, within fifty years, was to become probably the largest house plant business in the world—with Rochford's House Plants a household name.

Returning to Joseph Rochford, within eighteen years of setting up at Turnford he had built over thirty acres of glass and the business comprised several nurseries. It eventually reached almost seventy-six acres of glass, including a nursery at Slough and another at Waltham Cross, and became what is thought to be the largest glasshouse holding in the world.

After Joseph died, two of his sons, Joseph Patrick and Bernard, stayed in the firm. Joseph Patrick, or 'J.P.' as he was commonly called, ran the home nurseries at Turnford while Bernard, after being called to the Bar and deciding to give up the law in favour

of horticulture, built the 25-acre nursery at Slough and modern-
ised the nursery at Waltham Cross.

In later years, when the Lea Valley began to be taken over
for building, the firm expanded with a branch in the Isle of
Wight and yet another in Kenya.

CHAPTER ELEVEN

THE POUPARTS OF TWICKENHAM

DURING the eighteenth and early nineteenth centuries market gardening developed rapidly and on a large scale. In London, in particular, the process of selling market garden land for building and moving out to a bigger and often better holding went steadily on. As the markets of London became larger, many of the market suppliers began to find it worthwhile dividing their business into two sections—growing and marketing. The early market gardeners had produced the crop and also taken it to market to sell. But as the gardens went further out, this became increasingly difficult and it was often found better to have one member of the family permanently engaged in the marketing side and even living at the market during the week. As time went on, this was taken still further, with one market salesman setting up to sell the produce of a group of growers. Many famous wholesalers of today have their roots deep in the growing side of the industry.

Sometime during the eighteenth century, a Frenchman named Jean Poupart arrived in England. A Huguenot, he came to this country by his own choice, the persecution of Protestants on the Continent having by this time come to an end.

What Jean Poupart's profession was we do not know for certain. Probably he was a market gardener, like so many of his fellow countrymen. What is certain, however, is that in 1776 his son Jacques was in business as a market gardener on a piece of land which is now part of the Stamford Bridge ground of the Chelsea Football Club in London.

Maybe other members of the Poupart family came with Jean to England. If they did no doubt they, too, set up their market gardens for, by the middle of the nineteenth century, at least four Pouparts were selling their produce in London's markets.

Samuel, born in 1807, was the son of Jacques. His market

garden was at Battersea on Lord Spencer's estate. The farm-house stood close to where the Southern Region railway lines join between Clapham Junction and Battersea Park and the site was later commemorated as Poupart's junction and signal box.

In the early days of the ninteenth century, most of the market gardening was very much what can be termed spade husbandry. Intensive cultivation plus a tremendous amount of manure, mostly horse manure from the streets of London, together with a plenti-ful supply of cheap labour was the rule. J. C. Loudon in his *Encyclopedia of Gardening* has this to say about market garden-ing of that period :

> Some of these gardens are general, producing every description of culinary fruit and vegetables, hardy, exotic and forced, in demand; of which, as examples, may be mentioned the Earls-court garden, of upwards of 60 acres and with extensive hot-houses; and the Isleworth gardens. Other gardens near the metropolis are devoted chiefly to particular crops; as those at Mortlake, to asparagus; some at Battersea, to cabbage and cauliflower; at the Neats-houses to celery; at Deptford, to asparagus and onions; at Charlton and Plumstead, to peas etc. In some gardens attention is chiefly paid to forcing early and growing late crops; in others, as at Lambeth, exotic fruits, as pines and grapes are chiefly grown. At a greater distance from town, articles of easy carriage, as gooseberries, strawberries, asparagus, tart-rhubarb, sea kale etc. are leading articles; and in small gardens in the immediate vicinity of the metropolis nothing is sent to market; as watercress, radishes, parsley, herbs, and flowers are the chief articles grown, and they are sold in small quantities on the spot. The market-gardeners near sea ports direct their attention chiefly to the produce of cabbage, onions, turnips and such vegetables as are in demand as ship's stores.

Loudon goes on to describe other early nineteenth-century forms of commercial growing for market.

> Of *commercial gardens,* the lowest species are what are called *ploughed* or *farmers'* gardens. One or two are to be found near all large towns, and a number round London. They extend from fifty to one hundred and fifty acres or upwards, and are almost entirely cultivated by the plough and other agricultural implements. Their possessors are small farmers, and the chief

difference between this *farm-gardening* and common farming is that the green crops that intervene between the corn crops are more highly cultivated, and, instead of being consumed on the farm, are sent to market as culinary vegetables or food for stall-fed cows.

There were also, he says, market flower gardens and these were mostly close to London.

The second half of the ninteenth century saw London spreading fast. The railways, such as the one which took away part of the Poupart land, forced many market gardeners to move further away but in most cases they obtained good compensation from the railways and were able to set up again elsewhere. Some idea of the amount of this compensation is given in the account of a Mr Keaton whose rented land at Bermondsey had a seventy-five foot strip of track put through it by the Greenwich Railway Company. Mr Keaton claimed compensation because the arches of the viaduct made part of his market garden shady and the soot and smoke from the engines damaged his crops. He claimed £23,000 and got £15,000.

Another market gardener, Edwin Andrews, sued the Great Eastern Railway Company for damage by engine smoke to the produce of his nursery at Temple Mills Lane, Stratford. On this two-acre nursery he grew grapes and flowers successfully until 1880, when the railway ran some lines close by. Locomotives kept stopping in the neighbourhood and emitting volumes of thick black smoke. He claimed £500 damages and got it. Eight years later he claimed again and was awarded another £800.

One side effect of the arrival of the railways (and to a greater extent a little later on when motor transport took over from horses) was on the supply of manure from London. This went out by cart or barge to almost every market gardening area. Places such as Rainham in Essex were specially favoured by market gardeners because they were on a creek where the manure could be unloaded. It was even sent as far afield as Bedfordshire, where it was considered essential for maintaining the tilth of the light soil there.

But even if the horse population had not been declining, something would probably have had to be done about the trade in manure as it was becoming increasingly objectionable to the now more fastidious citizens of London.

Besides allowing market gardens to be set up much further from the big towns, the railways also speeded up supplies from abroad, which could now be landed at ports such as Dover and sent quickly to the big towns. The South Western and South Eastern Railway lines were the two principal carriers of foreign fruit. The South Western brought Spanish and Portuguese oranges, grapes, melons and nuts, while the South Eastern brought apples, pears, strawberries and nectarines from other parts of the Continent. The Brighton & South Coast Railway brought the produce of Jersey and the Dieppe area.

This increase in imports was not to the liking of market gardeners but it did extend the range and continuity of fruit, vegetables and flowers and was to the general advantage of trade. But not until refrigeration was introduced on ships and trains could produce really be imported quickly and in first-class condition. The first shipment of refrigerated produce was pears and green peas from Italy. By 1898, produce (in the form of apples) was coming from the other side of the world.

Through all these changing times the Pouparts continued to sell their own produce in Covent Garden market. By the 1890s William Poupart, who was probably Samuel's son, had left Bermondsey and after a few years at Kew was at Marsh Farm, next to the present Twickenham rugby ground. It is difficult to trace the market garden land owned or rented as it was being continually changed, either because of economic forces or because it was thought advisable to move to fresh land for cultivation purposes.

As William Poupart grew older, his elder son (also William) sold the produce in Covent Garden. But this William developed eye trouble and in 1892, at the age of sixteen, the younger son, John, took over the market work.

John proved keen and adept at selling and soon his enthusiasm, plus a reputation for honesty, brought him an increasing number of customers. Before long he was approached by other market gardeners to handle their produce. He accepted several and found business so successful that in 1895, while still only nineteen, he set up as a market salesman under the name of T. J. Poupart, the 'T' standing for Twickenham to distinguish him from another John Poupart who was market-gardening in Essex.

On 20 May that year John Poupart paid twenty-one shillings for a telegraphic address and three days later opened an account with the London County Banking Company in Henrietta Street. On 3 June, a shop at 51 Drury Lane was rented at eighteen shillings a week. On 18 June came the great day and a diary (still preserved in the family) recorded the first sale :

	J. Penfold and Sons				
6 pecks toms			£1	15s	0d
22 rims straws			£2	14s	6d
Commission	9s	0d			
Porters	1s	2d			
Carriage	3s	6d			
Toll	1s	2d		14s	10d
			£3	14s	8d

('Toms' are tomatoes and 'straws' strawberries.)

The business grew fast and more warehouse space was taken. Six years later a shop in the coveted Central Avenue of the Charter Market building in Covent Garden was rented.

John Poupart continued to handle the consignments of his grower friends, who were mostly from around the Hampton area in Middlesex. But he also sold the produce of the market gardeners in the fast developing Lea Valley north of London. Soon, the business became too much for one man and a partner was found in William Ravenhill, a buyer with whom John had done business for several years.

John Poupart was taking a financial gamble when he took a partner as the amount of his takings did not really warrant it and it is said that he had even to give up smoking for a while to help pay his way. However, things soon improved and after that he never looked back.

What was Covent Garden market like at the time when John Poupart started?

The old market of sheds and temporary buldings of Sarah Sewell's time had given way to a large Charter Market building and other special buildings for fruit and flowers. In 1828, an Act had been passed which gave the owner of the market, the Duke of Bedford, permission to pull down the old buildings and put up a modern market building. On 25 December 1828 a report in *The Times* read:

> Since the days of Hogarth until the last few months this great vegetable market (Covent Garden) has exhibited the same appearance of unsightly rows of dirty stalls, crammed, in most admired confusion, with the finest productions of the orchards and kitchen garden and the rarest specimens of the hothouse. Heaps of rotten fruit and putrid vegetables might be seen at any step you went and, in defiance of the market regulations, the tops of the stalls were usually filled with piles of baskets and all sorts of rubbish while the uncertain space allotted to rival greengrocers and fruiterers occasioned endless bickering, and added to the discomfort and annoyance of those who wanted to purchase. Thanks, however, to the 'march of intellect' and to the wise determination of the noble duke to whom the ground belongs those annoyances will shortly disappear and a new market more in accordance with the spirit of the age, and better adapted to the comfort and convenience of the seller and buyer will soon arise upon the ruins of the old.
> . . . The plan is intended to meet, as far as may be, the wishes of those who are most interested in the improvements, and that the old occupiers of the stalls will have nothing to complain of when the new shops are ready for their reception. . . . the improvements . . . have been undertaken in consequence of the repeated complaints which were made by the hotel-keepers and other respectable inhabitants of the parish in respect to the disorderly state of the market which had become a complete nuisance.

The new Charter Market designed by Charles Fowler had three parallel buildings running east-west with the centre building, Central Avenue or Grand Row, as the focal point. Central Avenue was a covered passage with small shops on either side. Each shop had its own cellar and a small upper room which could be lived in or used as an office. Most of the shops were let to people selling choice fruits and vegetables and, to begin with at least, almost all were retail shops.

Parallel with Central Avenue on the north and south were two other rows of shops, but these had no protection from the

Thomas Smith.

(below left) Sam Segar.

John Wills.

Mayland French garden.

Lettuce under cloches in 1908.

weather except a colonnade which formed a sheltered passage. The spaces between the three rows of shops were completely exposed except for one small section which had a roof.

Some of the larger market gardeners obtained sites within this new market building but most, among them to begin with, the Pouparts, had to sell their produce in the open against the competition of salesmen in the sheltered parts. To ventilate their grievances, they formed The Market Gardeners, Nurserymen and Farmers Association. In the list of members for 1851 to 1860 three Pouparts are mentioned—from Battersea, Bermondsey, and Walham Green.

The only shelter most of the market gardeners had at this time was a felt covering to their stand or a large umbrella, known as a gig or gingham. At one period, around 1860, the Duke of Bedford suggested that the Charter Market should be rebuilt on two floors so that everybody could then come in out of the wet and cold. But the market gardeners turned this down because they said that the tenants in the lower part would have a decided advantage over those above. 'It is well known,' said a memorandum to the Duke signed among others by Samuel Poupart, 'that public houses having a step had a disadvantage over those without one, and the same could apply to a market.'

Nothing however was done for about thirty years, by which time the congestion was so bad that a new building just had to be put up. This time E. M. Berry, the architect who had designed the Covent Garden Opera House, was called in and he produced the striking Floral Hall, in the form of a letter L and covered with a semi-circular roof of iron and glass. A dome of 50-foot span rose above the roof and the whole of the front was iron and glass. It cost over £30,000. As its name implies, it was first used for flowers, the demand for which was increasing rapidly. But so was the trade in imported fruit and after a few years the building was given over to fruit and the flower men had to look for other accommodation. In 1870, the Duke built a new Flower Market in the area flanked by Wellington Street, Russell Street and Tavistock Street. Then came the Jubilee Market in Tavistock Street, to be followed by a new vegetable market in Russell Street.

I

At the time John Poupart set up in business as a salesman the market was a busy and crowded place. Dickens, of course, knew the place well. In the 1860s he had an account with the firm of J. Rains in Central Avenue, and in one of the firm's old ledgers which came to light many years afterwards there were entries for items such as oranges, apples, pears, celery, chestnuts, seakale, sprouts, kale, grapes, asparagus, cucumbers, potatoes, artichokes, parsley, lemons and others. There were also entries for 'coat flowers'. Dickens settled his bills promptly, as 'Paid' appeared on each page with unfailing regularity. Dickens mentions Covent Garden in many of his books but the most factual description is in his *Dictionary of London* which was published from the offices of *All the Year Round* in Wellington Street, Covent Garden. The first edition in 1879 reads:

Covent Garden
No visitor to London should miss paying at least two visits to Covent Garden; one at early morning, say at 6 a.m.—the hour is an untimely one, but no-one would regret the effort that the early rising involves—to see the vegetable market; the other, later on, to see the fruits and flowers. All night long on the great main roads the rumble of the heavy waggons seldom ceases, and before daylight, the 'market' is crowded. The very loading of these waggons is in itself a wonder, and the wall-like regularity with which cabbages, cauliflowers, turnips, are built up to a height of some 12 ft is nothing short of marvellous. Between 5 and 6 o'clock the light traps of the greengrocers of the metropolis rattle, and all the streets around the market become thronged with their carts, while the costermongers come in in immense numbers. By 6 o'clock the market is fairly open and din and bustle are surprising indeed. Gradually the large piles of vegetables melt away. If it be summer-time, flowers as well as fruits are sold at the early markets. Then there are hundreds of women and girls among the crowd, purchasing bunches of roses, violets and other flowers, and then sitting down on the steps of the church, or of the houses round the market, dividing the large bunches into smaller ones, or making those pretty button-hole bouquets in which our London flower-girls can now fairly hold their own in point of taste with those of France and Italy. Even in winter, flower-girls find material for their little bouquets; for, thanks to steam, violets are brought from the Scilly and

Channel Isles, and even from the South of France and there is always a certain supply of hothouse flowers; so that there are many flower-girls who ply their trade at all seasons of the year. After 8 o'clock the market becomes quiet. The great waggons have moved off; the debris of cabbage leaves and other vegetable matter has been swept up and Covent Garden assumes its everyday aspect. And a very pretty aspect it is. The avenue is at all times of the year a sight, the shops competing with each other in a display of flowers and fruit such as can scarcely, if at all, be rivalled in any capital of Europe. In winter the aspect of the fruit shops changes somewhat, but not so much as might have been expected, for steam and heat have made it possible for the rich to eat many fruits, which formerly were in season but a month or two, all the year round. On each side of the main avenue are enclosed squares, and here the whole-sale fruit trade market is carried on. In winter there are thousands of boxes of oranges, hundreds of sacks of nuts, boxes of Hamburgh grapes and of French winter pears, barrels of bright American apples. At ten o'clock the sale begins; auction-eers stand on boxes and while the more expensive fruits are purchased by the West-end fruiterers, the cheaper are briskly bid for by the costermonger. Listen to the prices at which the fruit sells, and you wonder no longer at the marvellous bargains at which the itinerant vendors are able to retail their fruits, although, perhaps, you may be astonished when you remember the prices at which you have seen the contents of some of these boxes marked in fruiterers' shops. Outside the market there is almost always something to see. In winter a score of men are opening orange boxes and sorting their contents; in autumn dozens of women and girls are extracting walnuts from their juicy green outside cases; in spring-time the side facing the church is occupied by dealers in spring and bedding flowers, and the pavement is aglow with colour of flower and leaf, and in the early summer hundreds of women and girls are busily occupied in shelling peas. Country visitors will go away from Covent Garden with the conviction that to see flowers and fruits in perfection it is necessary to come to London.

Nearest *Railway Station,* Charing-cross (S.E. and Distr.). *Omnibus Routes,* Strand, St. Martin's-lane, and Holborn. *Cab Ranks,* Bedford-street and Catherine-street.

Life must have been interesting for John Poupart. By the time he had become a full-time salesman, the market was bulging at the seams. *Punch* in the 1880s kept having a go at what it christened 'Mud-Salad Market' and its owner the 'Duke of Mud-ford'. In one issue they even turned to 'poetry' :

HAMLET IN MUD-SALAD MARKET

O that these, too, too sordid sheds would fall,
Tumble and turn to heaps of builder's rubbish!
Or that parochialism had not fixed
Its veto 'gainst improvement! Mudford! Mudford!
How dirty, stale, damp and detestable
Seems to me all this muck-heap called a Market!
Fie on't, O fie! 'tis a true Sluggard's 'garden'
That runs to waste; things rank and gross in nature
Possess it merely. That we should look on this,
When care and cash—and not so much—could give us
So beautiful a Market, that to this
Were Tempe to a pig-run!

Nevertheless, plenty of business continued to be done. John Poupart's firm extended its activities considerably, the biggest move being at the turn of the century when it went into the rapidly growing imported fruit business.

By this time grapes were being imported from Holland, Spain, Portugal, Germany, France and the Channel Islands. Peaches came from France and the Channel Islands and even as far afield as America. There were also nectarines from France. From France, too, came green figs, though British growers were still producing large quantities, particularly in the Worthing area. Melons came from Lisbon, Cadiz and other parts of the Mediterranean, the Cadiz or Green-flesh being the most sought after.

Imported apples came from America (the Newtown Pippin being a favourite) in barrels each holding two or three bushels. France sent Calville Blanc, Reinette de Canada, and Court Pendu Plat. From Holland and Belgium came Brabant Bellefleur.

Pears came principally from France, the Channel Islands, Germany and Holland. Favourite varieties were Jargonelle, William's Bon Chrétien, Marie Louise, Duchesse d'Angoulême, Beurré Clairgeau and Louise Bonne of Jersey. They came in wooden cases holding from twenty to seventy fruits. Enormous specimens of Beurré Clairgeau and Belle Angevine pears came from Jersey and Guernsey. But California pears, mostly Easter

Beurré, were starting and these were to have a big influence on the trade a little later on.

Among the rarer fruits could be found prickly pears, pome-granates, custard apples, litchees, loquats and various nuts. And, of course, pineapples. The first St Michael pines arrived in 1867 when they were brought in still on the plants, and fifty fruits made £75. That year 427 fruits were sent. The figure in 1875 was 34,524 and by then other countries such as the Bahamas and America were also sending large quantities. Other imported fruits included at least twenty different kinds of citrus and there was a fast increasing trade in bananas.

Thus wholesalers handling vast quantities of both home-grown and imported produce became increasingly prominent in the markets of Britain, though side by side with them continued market gardeners who sold only the produce which they them-selves grew.

CHAPTER TWELVE

JOHN WILLS OF KENSINGTON

WITH the newly-developed glasshouse industry producing a much wider selection of exotic and out-of-season flowers, a new industry sprang up to sell them to the public. The modern florist shop was not known until the second half of the nineteenth century. Before that time, pot plants and cut flowers were sold from barrows or carts in the street. Greengrocers and fruiterers occasionally handled them but only if they were particularly cheap. Posies and bouquets were made up by girls who either took them from house to house or made them to order. The big increase in 'luxury' flowers soon brought into being shops which dealt in flowers alone. Many of the famous florists of today had their beginning around the end of the nineteenth century.

In the closing decade of the nineteenth century there were only about five high-class florist shops in London. Covent Garden market had retail shops in the Central Avenue, where they had been since the opening of the new Charter Market building in the 1820s, and all the other London fruit and vegetable markets had plenty of suppliers who brought pot plants, cut flowers and bedding plants to be sold both wholesale and retail.

The floral decoration business, however, goes back a very long way. In 1377, for instance, during the procession of the coronation of Richard III, it is reported that 'at the Little Conduit opposite Foster Lane, a castle with four turrets and a dome had been erected. In each turret was a maiden who blew golden leafs at Richard'.

During a procession of Queen Elizabeth from the Tower to Westminster in 1559, 'a poor woman made the Queen a gift of rosemary'. In 1685, at the coronation of James II, the procession was headed by the Royal Herb Woman 'with her six maidens strewing flowers and herbs'.

In the early days, flowers were sold by street sellers, many of whom had themselves grown the flowers in the immediate vicinity. The emphasis was on sweet-smelling herbs which were badly needed at times to mask the disagreeable odours caused by bad sanitation and such like. The nosegay, as its name implies, was originally for holding to the nose. Richard Weston in *Tracts on Practical Agriculture and Gardening*, published in 1769, advises growers that :

> . . . the flowers for nosegays are the quite common sorts, which require very little culture; they should in general be such as are sweet scented.

At first, flowers were little valued for their decorative use though no doubt from the earliest times most people gathered a few wild flowers to take indoors. The rich improved on this by having large gardens in which they cultivated out-of-season plants with which they could decorate their tables and surprise their guests.

In the time of Queen Elizabeth I rosemary, lavender, thyme, roses, marigolds, myrtle, stock and mignonette were the kind of flowers that the streetseller 'cried'. Many of these 'cries' became well known over the years. For example :

> Come buy my fine Roses,
> My Myrtles and Stock,
> My sweet-smelling blossoms
> And close-growing Box.

or :

> Here's your Sweet Lavender
> Sixteen sprigs to a penny—
> Which you will find my ladies
> Will smell as sweet as any.

Plants growing in pots are illustrated in medieval manuscripts such as the *Romance of Reynaud de Montauban* dating from the latter half of the fifteenth century and the prayer book of Juana of Castile, illuminated by Gheraert David about 1498. Carnations were the favourite pot plant in those days but Madonna lilies were grown in the same way.

During the seventeenth century, orange and lemon trees became fashionable and were grown in pots so that they could be taken indoors or out as conditions demanded. By 1722, Thomas Fairchild in *The City Gardener* is writing about what he describes as the 'common Bason of Flowers'.

> One may guess at the general love my fellow Citizens have for Gardening in the midst of their Toil and Labour by observing how much use they make of every favourable Glance of the Sun to come abroad and of furnishing their rooms or Chambers with Basons of Flowers and Bough-pots, rather than not to have something of the Garden before them.

But more intricate decoration was also being attempted. Box, privet, lilies, and orange trees in special containers, sometimes Delft ware, were being supplied by nurserymen such as Lee and Kennedy. Fairchild was in favour of these more elaborate decorations :

> The Chimneys which are generally dressed in Summer with fading Bough-pots might be as well adorned with living Plants, as I have observed at her Grace's the late excellent Duchess of Beaufort.

J. C. Loudon in his *Encyclopedia of Gardening* 1827 shows that specialisation in commercial flower growing was already in operation.

> Some gardens are noted for their roses; . . . others for growing the narcissus tribe, for geraniums, for cheap heaths, for mignonette, for forced flowers of all sorts. These gardens are not large; generally from one to a dozen acres.

By Victorian times, the demand for flowers and pot plants had grown but it had to fit in with the system of ornamentation that distinguished the Victorian era. The normal decoration of a Victorian drawing-room comprised plants growing in pots and of these amaryllis, aspidistra, palm, fern of many kinds, mignonette, geranium, marguerite and musk were the most popular. And in the corners of the room stood pampas grass or dried bullrushes.

Much of the developing glasshouse industry at the end of the nineteenth century was given over to producing these pot plants. Mignonette was once the most popular pot plant of all, yet fifty years later it was hardly heard of.

The Victorians were also fond of posies, bouquets and buttonholes and this started an industry for the production of short-stemmed cut flowers which were sent in large quantities to be distributed through the wholesale markets or sold direct from the nurseries. Bunches of mixed flowers were most in demand. The camellia and gardenia were favoured as buttonholes.

Towards the end of Queen Victoria's reign, longer-stemmed flowers became fashionable and have remained so ever since. The perpetual-flowering carnation became particularly popular for table decoration and was the flower chiefly responsible for taking the place of the pot plant as a table decoration. Eventually the cut-flower trade overtook that of the pot plant trade and within a few years huge glasshouses were erected for the growing of chrysanthemums, carnations, roses, daffodils, tulips and many other cut flowers. And the season of most kinds of flowers gradually increased until, with flowers such as roses, carnations and chrysanthemums, it became a year-round one.

The growing popularity of the cut flower also influenced the type of pot plant grown, so that the rather dull aspidistra, musk and mignonette had to make way for the brighter flowering azalea, cyclamen, cineraria, hydrangea and primula. It is hard to imagine that the later so-widely-grown *Primula malacoides*, for example, was only discovered growing wild in Tibet in 1907.

The demand for cut flowers also stimulated an industry based on the smaller flower. The daffodil, anemone, violet, ranunculus, aster, scabious, cornflower and the like began to be grown out of doors on a commercial scale in many parts of the country. And pot plants in a smaller form, particularly geranium, marguerite, genista, stock, cineraria, hydrangea and crassula, began to gain popularity.

Another welcome innovation was the window box, especially when big firms became interested in decorating their premises. The tawdry coloured glass flowers under a dome of glass which were a feature of graveyards began to go out of fashion and fresh flowers were put on graves.

Plants for planting out in gardens also became a large trade, though in the early days most had to be propagated almost entirely from cuttings as seed did not usually reproduce the habit and colour of the parent plant. The method of propagation of many of these plants was in water pans containing only pure washed sand and water, the cuttings being inserted in the sand and the pans placed in the full sun under glass.

Floristry as we know it today began about 1850. Before that there was probably not a florist shop in any town in the country. Yet people were quite flower conscious—particularly fashionable ladies. There is a theory that the start of the florist industry was due to the 'lady's maid'. These personal maids of the mistress of a house would demand from the gardener exotic blooms, and if the gardener could not meet their demands they went to nearby nurserymen for them. Great rivalry existed among the ladies' maids in dressing their mistresses and this applied, too, to the flowers they used. It was an age of lace frills, posy collars, silk-sheathed pins, ribbons and flounces, in all of which flowers played a great part.

It is thought that some of these ladies' maids having lost their jobs, possibly for reasons which prevented them from taking up a similar position elsewhere, turned their knowledge of flowers to good account and went to places like Covent Garden market where they earned a living making up posies, coronets, fans and body sprays which they would hawk in the fashionable districts or deliver to the house of any lady who might give an order.

The taste for flowers by the public in the mid-nineteenth century grew rapidly, according to a report in the *Gardeners' Chronicle* of July 1894, because :

(a)   the increase in population by the retirement of more citizens into suburban residences with gardens and conservatories.

(b)   greater affluence among the manufacturing and trading classes, enabling them to acquire and indulge in more refined taste.

(c)   the spread of education among the working class, which tended to create a taste for the beautiful.

(d)   country folk coming to the big towns looked on window plants as a connecting link with green fields.

(e)   the fashion of the age, which was to decorate tables and rooms and to put flowers on graves.

This taste for flowers increased the demand so much that in markets such as Covent Garden it became difficult to find room for all the pot plants and flowers. In Covent Garden, as we have seen, new buildings had to be put up to cater for the flower business and the scene presented by the Floral Hall, was described in C. R. Sims' *Living London*, 1904, as:

> . . . like the first bewildering glimpse of the transformation scene at a theatre. Against a background of broad-leaved palms and multitudinous flowerless plants, billowy clouds of snow-white blooms mingle with stretches of skyey-blue, shot through here and there with flaming reds and yellows and purples, all in a lavish setting of every shade and tinting of green. The blended fragrances within are suffocating sweet; the aisles of vivid, varied colour dazzle the eye almost as sunlight will; and strangely contrasted with their surroundings the salesmen, buyers, porters and others, might be merely scene shifters preparing the transformation scene, and the flower girls flocking about the cut flower stands might be blowzy, bedraggled fairies not yet dressed for their parts. Some of them are very old flower girls, and some of them very young; they are all keen bargainers, and go off with armfuls, or basketfuls, or apronfuls of scent and loveliness that, within an hour or two they will have wired into penny or twopenny bunches, and will be selling to spruce City men coming into town to their offices.

But these flower girls were only the lower end of the flower trade. The true florists were at the market first thing of a morning buying to meet whatever orders they had that day for weddings or other functions, or taking flowers and pot plants to stock their windows for the passing trade. A letter in the *Daily Telegraph* for 4 September 1869 complained about the trouble these new florists had in buying flowers in Covent Garden. The writer said there were two classes of retail dealers in flowers and both laboured under unfavourable conditions. Only the retail florists in the market itself (i.e. those in Covent Garden's Central Avenue) were allowed to buy before five, so that when the outsiders came all the best had gone.

The writer went on to say that thousands of wedding orders which could range from one guinea to 100 guineas a time needed to be done before 10 am and, particularly when the weather was warm, only those florists right on the spot in the market could do the orders without fear of the flowers deteriorating by the time of the wedding.

Who the first florist was to set up a shop to sell just flowers and to 'make-up' wreaths and bouquets and do floral decoration, is not known. Almost certainly it was a nurseryman, a grower of flowers and pot plants who, finding his nursery premises too cramped to deal with the fast increasing trade, decided to separate the growing and retail selling sides.

One man who did as much as anyone to set the fashion in floral decoration was John Wills from Chard, in Somerset, who came to London in 1867 to work at the Pineapple nursery of Arthur Henderson. This was situated close by Hall Road, just off the Edgware Road, and was one of the most famous nurseries of the day. Henderson had another nursery at Wellington Road, St John's Wood, which he kept mainly to provide plants to sell from his Pineapple nursery which was a show place and had many visitors. The Wellington Road nursery's chief claim to fame however is that in 1889 the Marylebone Cricket Club bought it (for £18,500) and still today Lord's Cricket Ground has its 'nursery end'.

By the 1880s, John Wills was general manager of the General Horticultural Company (John Wills) Limited which supplied vegetables, flower and agricultural seeds, garden implements and requisites, fruit trees, roses, floral decorations, bouquets, crosses, wreaths etc from Warwick House in Regent Street where the firm of Liberty is today. At that time the General Horticultural Company owned the Royal Exotic nursery in Onslow Crescent, Melbourne nursery at Anerley and a third establishment in Fulham.

By 1882, things were not going too well for John Wills, the General Horticultural Company was insolvent and he was glad to accept an offer from a Mr Segar to join him as partner and bring £1,000 into the business.

Sam Segar was in the horticultural business himself, having learnt the trade at the nursery of William Bull whose establishment stood in Chelsea on a site later occupied by Watney's brewery.

Joining John Wills, despite bringing £1,000 with him, was no sinecure for Sam Segar. The business, now Wills & Segar, was carried on from the impressive premises of the Royal Exotic nursery at Onslow Crescent, facing present-day South Kensington underground station. Here a group of greenhouses fronted by high palm houses were filled with plants of all description. On the left was the house in which the Segars lived and, facing the house and nursery, there was a space fenced around and known as Spike Island.

At the nursery, affairs were conducted in the grand manner. Heads of departments wore frock coats and top hats and escorted customers around the premises. The customer was met at the entrance by a man in uniform who, when it was wet, would have a large umbrella with him. Everything—even the door handles of the greenhouses—was kept well polished and the paths were swept each day.

These were the days of horses and carts. Wills & Segar kept eight horses and six vans in their own stables near the shop. Supplies of flowers came from their own nurseries and from Covent Garden market. It was also the days of grand functions and vast displays of flowers. The London season particularly was a time of intense activity for the florists and it was quite common for the staff to work from six in the morning till around ten at night. The season lasted about three months. In addition to the regular staff, men came in from the big houses in the country to work and learn the business at the same time, so that they could go back and continue, in a smaller way, providing plants for their own employer.

It was a period, too, of almost unlimited money among the gentry. At Buckingham Palace, for instance, in the days of Edward VII and Queen Alexandra, Wills & Segar kept a staff of four (three every morning and one permanent) just to look after the flowers while the King and Queen and foreign visitors were in residence. At one time, as many as six hundred vases were kept filled with flowers, besides the use of many hundreds of large pot plants that were so much the vogue. The story is told that at one period King Edward, deciding he must economize, went round inspecting the floral arrangements and finished up by taking away one small vase with three roses from Queen Alexandra's boudoir. The Queen indignantly ordered this to be put back and that was the end of the economy effort.

Wills & Segar were granted the royal warrant in 1886 and, following the example of the royal family, the gentry demanded more and more floral decorations. Trade was very good though there was one fly in the ointment—tradesmen sometimes had to wait a long time for their money. Many of the gentry would not deign to ask for estimates for anything and it was not uncommon for someone to come into the shop and buy its entire stock of flowers. But when it came to paying, it was a matter of waiting without daring to ask for the money. One well-known lord, for example, was a regular payer but always allowed seven years to elapse before he did pay.

In 1914, Wills & Segar bought four acres of the Royal nursery at Feltham in Middlesex. This was one of the nurseries of the famous firm, Veitch of Chelsea, perhaps the biggest and best of the nurserymen of the grand epoch. Their headquarters were in Chelsea and it was a huge concern embracing every branch of horticulture. The head of every department was a specialist in his subject and generally recognised as such in horticultural circles. The floral decoration department alone employed hundreds of gardeners during the London season, when every important social event was the occasion for lavish decoration with palms, ferns and flowers. There were departments for seeds, new and rare plants, fruit, forest trees and sundries. Veitch were one of the last who worked direct from their nursery without having a separate florist shop. So big was the concern that it was said that any gardener out of a job and who cared to come to London could be sure of finding employment there.

The founder of the firm, John Veitch, came from Jedburgh in Roxburghshire at the end of the eighteenth century to work as land steward for Sir Robert Ackland at Killerton in Devon. In 1808, he rented a piece of land near Killerton and started a nursery business which was to make the name and fortunes of five generations of his family. In 1832 John, his son James and his grandsons, Robert and James, moved to Exeter to start another business. In 1833 the firm, now James Veitch & Sons, bought out the old established nursery firm of Knight & Perry in King's Road, Chelsea and the younger James came to London to look after it. The new branch thrived and further grounds were added at Feltham, Langley and Coombe Wood near Kingston. The nurseries (Feltham specialised in seeds and vines, Langley in fruit trees and Coombe Wood in azaleas and rhododendrons) became a kind of gardening college where it was deemed a privilege to work.

The man largely responsible for the success of the Chelsea venture was Harry Veitch (Sir Harry as he later became). Born in 1840, he was educated at Exeter Grammar School and Altona University in Germany. He then trained with the seed firm of Vilmorin, near Paris. When he was thirty-one his father and his elder brother died, leaving him to manage the business. In 1914, the business was dissolved and Sir Harry refused to allow the name to be used by anyone else, though the branch at Exeter carried on as Veitch.

Four acres of the Veitch nursery at Feltham was bought by Wills & Segar and it says much for the Veitch standards of workmanship that fifty years later glasshouses built with their own labour were still in good condition. These glasshouses were wide and high, built to house palms and other tall plants. They were built of wood—strong, thick, durable pine. The packing shed, potting shed and two dwelling houses on the nursery also bore witness to the high standards set by the Veitch family.

Even after Wills & Segar took over the nursery, it continued to be run for many years on the rather grand Victorian lines. Charles Cordery, who was foreman of the nursery for thirty-five years from the time it was taken over, in the early days wore a frock coat and top hat. But the old-type palms and ferns had to give way to a more modern range of house plants, hydrangeas, ferns and so on with which to supply the florist shop of Wills & Segar, while anything surplus was sent to Covent Garden.

Even in 1939, however, the nursery had a collection of palms and other tall plants that would be worth a small fortune if they were in existence today. But under wartime regulations they literally came 'under the axe'.

By the turn of the century, florist shops were much in evidence and had indeed become the main outlet for most of the better quality plants and flowers grown by nurserymen, who supplied them direct or through the medium of the wholesale markets. Bouquets for weddings and other functions, wreaths, crosses, anchors, cushions and other floral emblems were made to order. Often the florist also undertook landscape work, jobbing gardening and the maintenance of window boxes. London florists, in particular, made a great name for themselves not only in the making of wreaths and bouquets but in the artistic decoration of banquet halls, theatres, reception rooms and the like.

Styles of decoration continued to change. Formerly, for example, bouquets were made in a round, flat and dumpy style having row after row of flowers arranged in circles round the centrepiece and usually finished off with a collar of fancy paper. Flowers were often sent to market with very short stalks so that the florist, to produce any effect at all, was obliged to mount them on wires.

One flower which did much to change this type of bouquet was the perpetual flowering carnation. This long-stemmed flower took the world of floristry by storm. And about the same time varieties and types of other flowers increased considerably. In the Victorian era during January, for example, there was little in colour except geraniums in scarlet and white, Roman hyacinths, lily of the valley and violets. Ferns were very important during the winter months. Flowering plants in pots were not numerous. Primulas were confined to *P. sinensis*. There were a few begonias of the fibrous-rooted kind. Carnations were the occasional Malmaison. But by the beginning of the twentieth century, not only was the carnation available all the year round but lily of the valley, forget-me-nots, marigolds and others were being forced out of season. Tulips, daffodils and most other bulb flowers also increased the length of their season. In iris, better varieties such as Wedgwood appeared. The dahlia, whose season had originally started in September, had its season advanced to July. The sweet pea increased its flowers on a stem from three to as many as six, and the rose became a year-round flower when the large glasshouse growers took over its cultivation.

Orchids did not come into prominence as a cut flower until about 1912, when scientific research at last produced a method of raising them in large numbers. But it was not until after the 1914-18 war that they became a regular feature of floristry. In recent years, flowers such as chrysanthemums and antirrhinums have considerably increased their season and this, together with a wide range of imported flowers, has given the modern florist an even greater scope.

CHAPTER THIRTEEN

THOMAS SMITH OF MAYLAND

TOWARDS the end of the nineteenth century, the back-to-the-land movement became popular and settlements were established where townspeople could work together in a co-operative venture. One who did a great deal for this movement was Joseph Fels, a wealthy American. Fels bought large tracts of land which he offered to public bodies for the settlement of such people. One of his gifts was 3,000 acres at Hollesley Bay in Suffolk, offered to the London Central (Unemployed) Body free for three years with the option of then buying it at the purchase price free of interest. Fels also bought a smaller place not far away, in Essex, where he installed a number of smallholders and put the enterprise in charge of an experienced manager to demonstrate just how such a co-operative venture should be run using 'French gardening' methods. The man he chose as manager, Thomas Smith, was a former printer who had given up everything to become an horticulturist.

Thomas Smith's father was a Lancashire tinplate worker with a Scottish-Irish wife who brought up a family of five at Warrington and Manchester. Thomas, born in 1857, took his first job at the age of nine in a glasshouse—not a horticultural glasshouse but a place where, in this case, wineglasses were made. He worked a six-hour shift every day for four shillings and sixpence a week. The family moved and Thomas had to take a lower-paid job in a rope-walk at half-a-crown a week.

Looking for more money, Thomas next found work with the *Warrington Examiner* at six shillings a week and this lasted for one and a half years at the end of which, having become attached to the print trade, he signed on as an apprentice with John Barnes, printers, of Manchester. After completing the six years of his apprenticeship he was made a journeyman at thirty-five shillings a week. He married in 1879 and set up on his own as a small printer.

After seventeen years of married life, at the age of thirty-eight and with two children—a girl of fourteen and a boy of thirteen— Smith decided to give up his printing business and a comfortable home and devote his life to horticulture.

Smith's feelings about the country were somewhat romantic and can perhaps be summed up in those lines of Goldsmith which he was later to quote in one of his books :

> Ill fares the land, to hast'ning ills a prey,
> Where wealth accumulates and men decay.
> Princes and lords may flourish or may fade;
> A breath can make them as a breath has made,
> But a bold peasantry, their country's pride,
> When once destroyed can never be supplied.

More directly, Smith was influenced by a socialist weekly, *The Clarion*, which in 1895 published a series of articles about a man who was maintaining himself and his family 'beyond his expectations' on three acres of land in Essex.

When Smith made up his mind to do the same, he sold his printing business for £800 and went off to Essex. He bought eleven acres of land at Mayland, near Althorne, and built a cottage which he called 'The Homestead'. The eleven acres were 'five of red pasture and six of weed-grown and wet arable'. He started with a few cows, pigs and poultry but soon found himself in financial difficulties. A lawyer friend in Manchester lent him money on a mortgage and he used it to plant fruit and lay out a kitchen garden.

The farmers in the area regarded these 'back-to-the-land' towns- folk as something of a joke and gave them little help. Smith was forced to go back temporarily to the printing business to earn money to carry on in his new occupation. He took a job in Manchester, but his wife found it too difficult to carry on at Mayland on her own, so after six months he returned.

He now took every odd job he could find to try and make ends meet. Meet they eventually did and as soon as he had accumu- lated a little capital he built two glasshouses each 50 ft by 20 ft in which he grew tomatoes and cucumbers. The glasshouses proving the most profitable of his ventures, he sold off the cattle and poultry and built some more, as well as extending his crops to include lettuce and early strawberries.

He then accepted an offer from Joseph Fels to manage a near-by co-operative holding and to learn the intensive culture system better known as 'French gardening'. One of the apostles of this system was Prince Kropotkin who, in his *Fields, Factories and Workshops*, proclaimed :

> While science devotes its chief attention to industrial pursuits, a limited number of lovers of nature and a legion of workers whose very names will remain unknown to posterity have created of late a quite new agriculture, as superior to modern farming as modern farming is superior to the old three fields system of our ancestors. . . . They smile when we boast about the rotation system having permitted us to take from the field one crop every year, or four crops each three years, because their ambition is to have six and nine crops from the very same plot of land during the twelve months. They do not understand our talk about good and bad soils because they make the soil themselves. . . .

And he went on :

> Fifty years ago the 'culture maraîchère' was quite primitive. But now the Paris gardener not only defies the soil—he would grow the same crops on an asphalt pavement—he defies climate. His walls which are built to reflect light, and to protect the wall-trees from the northern winds, his wall-tree shades and glass protectors, his frames and pepinières have made a real garden, a rich southern garden, out of the suburbs of Paris. He has given to Paris the 'two-degrees less of latitude' after which a French scientific writer was longing; he supplies his city with mountains of grapes and fruit at any season; and in the early spring he inundates and perfumes it with flowers. But he does not only grow articles of luxury. The culture of plain vegetables on a large scale is spreading every year. . . .

The system was quite simple, said Kropotkin :

> . . . its very essence is first, to create for the plant a nutritive and porous soil, which contains both the necessary decaying organic matter and the inorganic compounds; and then to keep that soil and the surrounding atmosphere at a temperature and moisture superior to those of the open air. The whole system is summed up in these few words.

This over-simplification was the sort of thing to appeal to people who knew little of horticulture. Intensive gardening had been practised in France for several centuries. Claude Mollet, the first gardener to Louis XIII at the beginning of the seventeenth century, was a great exponent of it and wrote about it in *Theatre du Jardinage* published in 1700. Another French gardener, La Quintinye, whose *Instruction pour les Jardins Fruitiers et Potagers* was published in 1690, mentions how he produced out-of-season produce such as asparagus in December, lettuce in January and strawberries early in April.

Intensive cultivation had, of course, been practised in Britain but never on so large or so thorough a scale as in France. A report on the French system in 1904 said that the Paris gardens averaged from three to ten acres. Each garden had a large number of frame lights about three feet square resting on boards twelve inches above the soil. Reed mats were used to cover the lights, and bell glasses or cloches were also used on a considerable scale.

The Paris *maraîchers* exported a large amount of produce every year to Britain and it was this that made the British growers increasingly aware of the system. As many as 5,000 crates of lettuce, each containing thirty-six heads, came to England daily during the season, which ran from a week before Christmas right up to March. Small carrots came at the rate of 500 crates daily, asparagus 100 crates, turnips 100 crates and celeriac fifty crates. No wonder the British grower was worried.

In 1905, a party of growers from the Evesham area went to Paris to see how the system worked. A few months after they came back a French garden was set up at Bengeworth in Worcestershire by a Mr Idiens and then carried on by J. N. Harvey. In 1906, this enterprise occupied three-quarters of an acre, laid out in a series of narrow beds. On top of the beds were placed 300 framelights and large numbers of bellglasses. The crops grown were lettuce, radish, cauliflower, turnips, cucumbers and melons. Water pumped into a tank from the River Avon supplied the large quantities required in spring and early summer. Within a few years there were 2,000 lights and 4,000 bellglasses and the return was around £600 an acre.

By the time Joseph Fels and Thomas Smith became interested, the movement was in full swing. The two men made a trip to Paris and were sufficiently impressed to engage a French *maraîcher* and his family to come to Essex.

The *maraîcher* taught Smith several new things. For example, he always raised three separate batches of melon seedlings but threw away two of the batches. His explanation was that the young melon plants had to be of a certain stage of growth at transplanting, neither too old nor too young, and that by having three lots he could choose those which were just right. Smith thought it a rather expensive way of doing things. The *maraîcher* used 1,200 tons of stable manure on the two acres. Most of it went into the making of the hot beds. As soon as the first hot beds had settled down to the required temperature, three crops were set out on each bed. For example, sown radish and carrots were followed by lettuce plants raised in a propagating house and carefully selected to be of one size and free of disease.

When the French garden had developed into a profitable working concern, Smith decided to write a book describing the methods. It came out as *French Gardening* by Thomas Smith, F.R.H.S., supervisor of the Fels Small Holdings, manager of the Fels Fruit Farm, Windmill Nurseries and French Garden, Mayland, Essex. It was published by Joseph Fels at 39 Wilson Street, Finsbury E.C. in conjunction with Utopia Press, Worship Street, Finsbury in 1909. It had a foreword by Prince Kropotkin and in a letter which Joseph Fels sent to editors asking for the book to be reviewed he said he wanted to see the book—

. . . as widely circulated as possible, because I am advised that it is the most practical thing yet prepared and only good can come of honest writing on what you are no doubt aware is a difficult subject.

He added, 'I have no financial interest in the book.'

In his preface, Thomas Smith said that no attempt had been made to advertise the Mayland French garden but that nevertheless there had been many enquiries as to how it was run. It was for this reason that he had decided to write the book. He also wanted to warn the public, he said, about statements on French gardening which were not consistent with the actual facts and which gave people the impression that this method of gardening was like the discovery of a gold mine. He went on :

> The impression conveyed to the public by such wild and misleading statements is calculated to do an immense amount of mischief. . . . There is not the slightest doubt that the French system of gardening is in various ways an improvement on customary methods, and that extraordinary crops can be taken from comparatively small areas; but although the ultimate net profits, after a garden is brought into a state of efficiency, will doubtless be satisfactory—providing present prices are maintained—they in no way approach those the public has been led to expect.

French gardening, he continued, should only be carried on by people with plenty of capital and he warned smallholders that they should go very carefully. At Mayland, he said, they had grown early salads, vegetables and canteloupe melons of the finest quality and sold them in Covent Garden at prices equal to, and frequently higher than, those paid for imported produce.

Smith went on to say that English glasshouse growers were among the best in the world, especially for grapes, peaches, melons, cucumbers, tomatoes and cut flowers. What could be done in big glasshouses could be done, he maintained, in small glass frames using hot beds or hot-water pipes. A garden laid out on a commercial scale of two acres and well managed, should, when in working order, show a profit at the end of three years. Until then the profit would be meagre or none at all. A large amount of capital had to be sunk in equipment and large sums expended annually on labour and manure. There were also railway charges, depreciation of plant, interest and capital. Also some training in gardening was essential.

> Many people actually think that by reading a book and getting a few verbal explanations they can forthwith undertake, without further preliminary, this highly specialist business, with full expectation of making a living. Such expectation is foolish and must end in disappointment and disaster.

Thomas Smith was not the man to be falsely optimistic; he had seen too many bad times himself.

The French garden at Mayland continued to do well for a

time. But soon Smith was finding that the ways of the *maraîchers* were not always acceptable. They liked, for example, to do quite a bit of private selling on the side, a practice which Smith very much frowned upon.

One day the *maraîcher* at Mayland came to Smith and said that his wife was homesick for France. Smith gave them a fortnight's holiday with all expenses paid. They never came back and it was found afterwards that they had taken another, better-paid job near Brighton. Two younger Frenchmen were engaged but did not last long. After that, Smith used members of his own staff until the 1914-18 war, when labour became so scarce and manure so difficult to obtain that the French garden had to be discontinued. For the same reasons, other French gardens up and down the country were given up.

Meanwhile, Smith carried on looking after the smallholdings and doing a good deal of lecturing. He then decided to turn the lectures into a book and, as a former printer, resolved to print it himself. He spent £250 in setting up a small printing office, which he used for general printing as well as for the book. He bought only enough type to set up eight pages at a time, so he worked out a system of doing four pages and sending them to London to be electrotyped while he worked on the next four. When a forme of four pages came back, he distributed the type and carried on.

He decided to confine his book to vegetables, putting into it all that a smallholder needed to know 'from initial dealings with the soil, through all the ramifications of production to the final disposal of the produce'. To begin with, he wrote by hand but, finding this 'tedious and time-wasting', he then set the text straight into type except for the tables and plans. The work took him several months 'whenever I could spare an hour or two, sometimes during the day but more often at night after outside work was done'. At last the book was finished and given the title *The Profitable Culture of Vegetables*. Smith then set out to find a publisher. He says, 'I don't suppose there was ever an author who went in search of a publisher with his book already set up and with the plates all ready for the press'.

He had no knowledge of which publishers to approach but

THE
PROFITABLE CULTURE
OF
VEGETABLES,

FOR MARKET GARDENERS, SMALL HOLDERS, AND OTHERS.

BY

THOS. SMITH,

F.R.H.S.,

**Manager of the Fels Fruit Farm and the Mayland French Garden.
Author of " French Gardening."**

FULLY ILLUSTRATED.

LONGMANS. GREEN AND CO.,
39. PATERNOSTER ROW. LONDON.
NEW YORK, BOMBAY, AND CALCUTTA.
1911.

The title-page of Thomas Smith's book on vegetable culture.

eventually settled terms with Longmans. The book appeared in 1911 and, with several revisions, has become a classic in its field.

Sometime during this period Smith had amalgamated his own holding, The Homestead, with the other smallholdings and ran them together. But the co-operative effort was not going too well. Some of the members were beginning to be dishonest in their dealings, and there was also a certain amount of 'topping-up' of produce sent to the markets. It was decided to sell as much produce as possible retail and so try to obtain better prices. Three light, horse-drawn lorries were used and the district was divided into three parts, a lorry and driver being appointed to each.

For a time everything went well but gradually it was discovered from the accounts that retail selling did not bring in the extra profit it should have done. The theory behind it was all right but it was found that there was systematic thieving from the lorries at night, and this became so widespread and was so difficult to check that the retail business had to be closed down.

Dishonesty was also rampant in other spheres. Women working in the fields would hide fruit and vegetables under babies in their prams. Others had special pockets made in the bottom of their skirts. One man and his wife were found to be doing a regular retail trade with stolen tomatoes. One night twenty bushels of apples, ready for despatch to market, disappeared, and some nights whole trees of fruit were cleared.

To retrieve the situation, another scheme was tried. Produce was sent by rail to regular private customers in London. Besides fruit and vegetables, eggs, chickens, butter, young pork, mushroom, hares, rabbits and honey were provided, but it was soon evident that the cost of transport was far too high for a profit to be shown.

While all this was going on, Smith received many distinguished visitors who were interested in the 'back-to-the-land' movement. They included George Lansbury, Rider Haggard, Prince Kropotkin, Sidney and Beatrice Webb, Lord Carrington, Keir Hardie and many others. 'Some came from mere curiosity' says Smith, 'some genuinely desirous of learning, some mere cranks'.

And there were plenty of visits from Joseph Fels, the rather eccentric millionaire who had put up the money for the smallholdings in the first place. Fels eventually became disheartened with the whole project and sold off many of the smallholdings. When it came the turn of the French garden, Smith offered to buy and became the owner for £2,000.

After 'six or seven years of stress, turmoil and hard work from which practically the whole profit I had gained was experience' Smith and his family returned to The Homestead where plenty more work awaited him. He carried on as a successful market gardener on his own account until he went into semi-retirement at Westcliff at the age of seventy-five, leaving a manager in charge. After his wife's death in 1939, he moved to various places but, at 96, decided to go and live with his son and grand-daughter in Northumberland.

In 1950, the Royal Horticultural Society gave him a Veitch Memorial gold medal 'in recognition of the work you have done for horticulture and in particular as the author of that magnificent text-book *The Profitable Culture of Vegetables.*'

Thomas Smith died in 1955 at the age of 98. But *The Profitable Culture of Vegetables* remains to this day a classic of commercial horticulture and certainly the only gardening book to have been 'written' and set up in type in a potting shed.

CHAPTER FOURTEEN

ALFRED SMITH OF FELTHAM

THAT branch of horticulture known as market gardening has, through the ages, been the least publicised of any. The men who introduced new plants, designed gardens, sold plants to the public, became head gardeners to famous men and so forth have often been written about. But over several centuries men who have done great work in providing the population of our big cities with vegetables, fruit and flowers have held the stage for a few years and disappeared into obscurity. By the end of the nineteenth century, market gardening had developed into a huge industry around London, though it had gradually moved further away from the City itself. One large section had settled in west Middlesex from where the London markets were supplied daily.

Around the Feltham and Hampton areas of west Middlesex, large expanses of good growing land were still to be found at the turn of the century and though some distance out of London it was not too far to be reached by the horse-drawn vehicles which were still the main means of conveyance for local horticultural produce.

One of the biggest and best market gardeners in this area was Alfred William Smith who lived and worked there for fifty years and at his zenith possessed over 1,000 acres of vegetables, fruit and flowers, as well as one of the biggest ranges of glasshouses to be found anywhere in the world.

A. W. Smith was a man 'of extreme modesty, deeply but silently religious, did not drink or smoke and never swore'. This description comes from his foreman, Alfred Lucas, who was with him for fourteen years and who, in later life, set down on paper much of what he could remember about his former employer.

Smith left school at the age of nine and from then onwards claimed never to have had time to read or take a holiday. He supervised everything himself wherever possible and for most of his life went regularly to market to sell the produce, as well as doing a full day's work on the farm. He had no hobbies and seldom mixed with other growers. He rarely praised his staff and treated them with an iron discipline. No smoking, drinking or swearing were allowed and to be late on the job could mean dismissal. Alfred Lucas tells the story of when he wanted to get married and managed to obtain half a day for the wedding and honeymoon. The following morning, due back at the farm at six, he arrived three minutes late after cycling three and a half miles. Smith was waiting, watch in hand. 'Boy' he said (and this was to his foreman) 'if you can't get here to time, you had better look for another job'.

Smith worked hard all his life. In his youth, he was with his father, Henry Smith of Feltham, also a market gardener, and until he was married he received no wages or holidays. When he started in business for himself he had one horse, some second-hand farm implements and forty acres of fruit. When his father retired, he took over his business as well and paid his father £3,000 (in instalments). Later, he also took over the land of a brother.

Perhaps Smith was lucky (for his business) to be living at a time when jobs were few and competition for them very keen. The average wage for a man was then eighteen shillings for a sixty-two hour week, and for a woman twelve shillings. Overtime for the man was fourpence per hour and the women twopence halfpenny. Foremen got twenty-five shillings a week, plus a cottage, but they had to work long hours and earned no overtime. (In 1890 there was a strike of over 600 men in the Chiswick/ Richmond area close to Hampton when they demanded fourpence halfpenny an hour normal, sixpence an hour after ten hours and no work after four o'clock on a Saturday.)

Unpunctuality was punished by a fine. If a worker was absent when the bell rang for work he was fined a quarter of an hour's pay. Fines were also imposed for what might be considered quite trivial things—to break the head of a brussels sprout while picking would mean a fine of a halfpenny; to eat a plum without permission incurred the penalty of sixpence.

Smith was a shrewd grower. He liked to keep the acreage of his regular crops static and not to increase it to suit the season or conditions at the markets. The only time he would increase acreage was after a bad season for prices, banking on the fact that most growers after a bad season would grow less.

He manured heavily—for most vegetables at a rate of fifty tons to the acre. The land was always kept in a state of high fertility, with the result that he did not have to worry much about rotation of crops and could often grow the same crop on the same land for several years in succession. His routine crops included spinach, onions, leeks, sprouts, savoys, cabbage, beetroot, parsnips and potatoes while crops such as strawberries, rhubarb, apples, pears and plums occupied the same piece of land for several years. In addition, there was a large number of glasshouses producing out-of-season crops.

With the green crops, the year began with spinach which was drilled early in spring. This crop finished in early May and the cleared ground and the remaining land was planted with brussels sprouts, savoys, cauliflowers, kale and broccoli, all of which had been raised in protected seed-beds.

Brussels sprouts were one of the most important crops. They were grown in rows three feet apart and the plants two feet apart in the rows. As soon as the plants were established, the space between the rows was horse-hoed, after which hand-hoeing was carried out between the plants. When the plants were about eighteen inches high they were earthed up. Soot was applied during dry spells to prevent attacks of green fly. When mature, the sprouts were gathered from six o'clock in the morning until late afternoon, whatever the weather. Then the pickers would move to a shed on the field to sort and pack what they had picked. This took another four hours. During the winter, it was sometimes so cold that the women froze to the sorting table and had to untie their aprons to get free. After a wet day they had to stay for hours in their wet clothes. And all this for twopence halfpenny an hour! The system in the packhouse was to turn the sprouts out on to the sorting table, separate the 'tight' sprouts from the remainder and remove any yellow foliage. These 'tight' sprouts were put into half-bushel baskets; the poorer quality and larger 'blown' sprouts went into bushels. The half-bushels were finished off by packing the sprouts one by one round the rim of the basket in the form of a pyramid until a single sprout remained at the top to form the apex.

Savoys were planted in rows two feet apart with the plants eighteen inches apart in the rows and then treated much like the brussels sprouts, except that they were not earthed up and soot against greenfly was rarely necessary.

Cauliflowers were spaced two feet by two feet and when half grown were earthed up and cultivated in the same way as the brussels sprouts. During hot weather, the curds were protected by breaking leaves over them.

Curly kale was planted two feet by eighteen inches, and sprouting broccoli a little wider. Neither the kale nor the sprouting broccoli was marketed until after Christmas and were kept going until April.

Spring cabbage was drilled during the last week in July and was ready for planting out in September and October. Planting distance was eighteen inches by fifteen inches.

Many varieties of cabbage were grown, the favourites being Early Offenham and Meins No 1 for early outdoor work, Enfield Market for later outdoor and Hurst's First and Best for cabbages grown in glasshouses. After planting, the cabbages were allowed to become established, then the ground between the rows would be horse-hoed and the space between the plants hoed by hand. Further cultivation was left until after Christmas, when hoeing took place every two or three weeks. The earliest plants were encouraged to heart by tying with raffia. The first tied cabbages usually reached the market about the end of February and cabbage in general kept on until well into July.

Winter spinach was sown as near as possible to 12 August and thinned out to one plant every six inches in rows twelve inches apart—just wide enough to allow a pony-drawn hoe to get through safely. As soon as the leaves were large enough, they were picked and this picking was carried on regularly until the following May or June when the plants went to seed.

Some twenty to thirty acres of Tripoli spring onions were grown annually. This crop, like winter spinach, was sown as near as possible to 12 August. It was drilled in rows twelve inches apart and kept clean by hand-hoeing and weeding. The following February, the onions were pulled out in handfuls and bunched in the field, using a small table which was fitted with two wheels in front. The women loosened the onions in the soil with a fork while others pulled them out, shook off the loose soil and laid them on the ground. Another woman picked up the onions and took them to the sorting table, where the foreman's mate bunched together the correct number before handing them to the foreman himself who was responsible for making them into a fan-shaped bunch tied with a rod of withy. The bunches were washed with a scrubbing brush and sold in the market by the dozen or five-dozen bunches. A buncher was expected to do 120 an hour and the best could get up to 150.

Leeks were usually sown under a frame in late February and early March and planted out in May and June. Varieties were Musselburgh and The Lyon. Before planting, the roots and tops were trimmed a little and then planted loose and six inches apart by dibber. The were dug, 'skinned' and tied seven or eight to a bunch with a rod and when finished resembled a hand, each leek standing away from its fellows like fingers. The top of the bunch was cut level and all the bunches washed clean.

Root crops were beetroot, parsnips, turnips, mangolds, potatoes and Jerusalem artichokes.

Beetroot was the premier root crop and was almost entirely Cheltenham Green Top. It was sown in rows fifteen inches apart and thinned out to six inches apart. The foliage was taken off before marketing and used as food for cattle or ploughed in as green manure. The beetroot was lifted by the end of November, sorted into large, best and smalls and the various heaps were then covered with the discarded foliage until the beetroot could be clamped. The clamps for the beetroot were in high but sheltered places and were made by digging out the soil to about twelve inches over an area some five feet in diameter. The bottom of this shallow pit was covered with straw and the beetroot arranged on this base in a ridge-shaped heap. The heap was then covered with straw and the soil which had been taken out was put back on top to give protection from the weather. Funnels of straw were made in the sides of the clamp for ventilation. Potatoes, parsnips and mangolds were also clamped in similar fashion.

Field peas were grown without sticks in rows about three feet apart. Hoeing was carried out regularly until the peas showed bloom when they were earthed up by drawing the loose soil about half way over the haulm and so almost laying the peas flat. In a few days the peas straightened up and showed great benefit from the earthing up. As the crop was picked, so the haulm was turned first to one side and then to the other so that the sun could get at both sides. Smith was a firm believer in sunshine as a source of flavour and tenderness.

The peas were picked mostly by gangs of gipsies who were taken on to relieve the regular women who concentrated on the more responsible business of harvesting the soft fruit. The gipsies were paid sixpence a bushel for pea picking but no half-ripe peas were allowed to be included.

Cos lettuce and any long lettuce were tied about four days before pulling for market.

The strawberry season ran from the third week in June until the first week in August and, except on Sundays, everyone worked an eighteen-hour day from three o'clock in the morning until nine at night. No work was done on a Sunday unless absolutely essential for Smith was a religious man who believed in the full observance of the Sabbath. Gangs of pickers, up to 200 in a single gang, were each in charge of a foreman. One picker went to each row. Fruit had to be gathered by the stalk only and leaves were picked separately to be used as decoration and protection for the fruit in the punnets. Full punnets were taken twelve at a time on a head-board to the sorting table at the end of the field. At this table the 'leafing' girls prepared the punnets with about four leaves to each punnet to make a complete 'bed' for the fruit.

The sorters graded the fruit on a table into bests, seconds, thirds and specks, handling them always by the stem only. When full, the punnets, after weighing, were packed into cases each holding thirty-six punnets and each layer was covered with freshly picked leaves. The first load caught the 4.7 am train from Twickenham to Waterloo, where a van was waiting to rush the fruit to Covent Garden market. The second load went on the 6 am train from Hounslow and the third and fourth soon afterwards from Feltham.

As we have seen, the tomato began to become popular with the Lea Valley growers towards the end of the nineteenth century and men like Joseph Rochford were building large glasshouses to accommodate the crop. A. W. Smith, though not in the Lea Valley, was one of the first to recognise the potentialities of this crop, and anticipated the demand by putting up twenty glasshouses covering ten acres in which to grow them. This venture proved one of the most profitable he ever undertook. The average wholesale price for tomatoes in the early season was around four shillings a box of twelve pounds. Smith's average crop was four pounds per plant, so that every plant brought in about 1s 4d. (Later, due to increased imports, the price of tomatoes dropped to as low as 1s 6d for twelve pounds.)

The ten acres of glass were put up one winter ready for spring planting. No outside builder, engineer or surveyor was employed and no-one on the staff had much knowledge of the building of glasshouses. But by using what knowledge was available and a great deal of common sense, the houses were built and built well.

To supply the houses with water a 50-foot high tower with a tank was designed, made and erected by the farm staff. A well was sunk and when this proved insufficient a reservoir was added. The timber for the houses had to be cut and painted with one coat of priming and two coats of white paint. All the paint was mixed on the premises from the best white lead, linseed oil and turpentine. Hundreds of bags of putty were needed. The brickwork of the houses was also done by the staff.

Smith was in advance of his time in not using any more timber in a house than absolutely necessary because of the shade it cast on the growing crops. Ventilators with outside levers of the type invented by Joseph Rochford of the Lea Valley were used.

When completed, the ten houses, each 600 feet long, were probably the largest block in the world. They cost £13,500.

The first crop of tomatoes taken from the houses did not turn out too well. Blaming the soil, Smith then bought 200,000 twelve-inch pots and filled them with surface soil from seven acres of land he had ploughed up on another part of the farm. In the following season, by growing the tomato plants in these pots and mulching with two inches of rotted manure, he doubled the crop.

Smith was a keen believer in farmyard manure and used over 200 tons a week on his various holdings. No chemical fertilisers were entertained. At one period he had a contract with several London mews to clear their manure each week. He first used his own horse wagons returning empty from market to carry the manure, but later put in a railway siding at Feltham and had his own goods wagons.

At first the tomatoes were watered at the roots by hose-pipe but later overhead irrigation was installed and proved very satistory. Varieties of tomato grown included Sewell's Beauty, Up-to-Date, Chemin Rouge, Challenger, Hillside Comet and Holme's Supreme. Of these, Sewell's Beauty held the record for cropping with an average of four pounds a plant for tomatoes grown in a cold house. Hillside Comet was rather too large a fruit for market, but was so regular in size that forty-eight to a box almost invariably weighed twelve pounds.

Another crop at Feltham was mushrooms and Smith was one of the first to grow them successfully under glass without any shading. Previously he had grown them in large sheds with wood and felt roofs and heated by two rows of four-inch pipes which went round the entire building. He used tons of manure a year for his mushrooms, which were graded into 'broilers' and 'cups'.

Mint was also grown on a large scale both outside and under glass. For outdoors, the practice was to manure heavily then plough to about six inches. The mint was planted six inches apart in rows nine inches apart. For the first year the ground was kept clean by hand hoeing, then mulched again and the second year crop marketed by pulling it and bunching with the roots on. This thinned out the beds, giving plenty of room for the plants to carry on for a third year.

Under glass mint roots (as opposed to plants) were used and

covered with two inches of soil which was then flattened with a spade. Heat was given to part of the crop to bring it to maturity before the remainder.

The fruit plantations at one period extended to 400 acres and it was all hand-forked during the winter and any serious weeds taken away and burnt. The young plants and trees for the plantation were all grown in Smith's own plant nursery. Here the fruit trees were budded or grafted as required and surplus trees were sold by public auction. The two rootstocks most used for apples were crab and Paradise. Dessert varieties of apples grown included Cox's Orange Pippin, Worcester Pearmain, King of the Pippins, Early Julyan, Beauty of Bath and Duchess Favourite. Cookers were Stirling Castle and Ecklinville Seedling.

Of dessert apples, Cox was considered the best for flavour, though Worcester Pearmain, too, was delicious when eaten straight from the tree. Early Julyan could be used for both eating and cooking and was a heavy cropper. King of the Pippins was an excellent late apple if kept until mature. Beauty of Bath was of 'beautiful flavour and exquisite aroma, though a doubtful cropper'. Duchess Favourite was a very sweet apple.

The most popular cooking apple was Stirling Castle which gave a wonderful crop when grown on Paradise rootstock. Ecklinville Seedling did best on crab stock; it had a thin skin and did not travel well, though for quality in cooking there was nothing to touch it.

Of pears, Duck Egg, Hessle, William's Bon Chrétien, Calabasse and Pitmaston Duchess were the main varieties. William's Bon Chrétien was regarded as the best flavoured of all the pears grown on the farm.

Enormous quantities of plums were grown. River's Early Prolific, a black plum, was ready at the end of July. Gisborne, a yellow plum, was of inferior quality but as it flowered late it often escaped late frost and therefore could have a full crop when other varieties were having a short one. It was ready at the end of July and was a good cooker. Prince of Wales was a choice dessert plum but the trees had a habit of dying suddenly for no apparent reason. Victoria was already making a name for itself as the best of the all-round plums, and was followed in season by the darker Pond's Seedling. Czar and Orleans were ready in mid August and Monarch, a black plum, came in late September.

Gooseberries were Crown Bob, Lancashire Lad, Whinham's Industry, White Lion and The Sulphur. The first three turned red when ripe, whereas White Lion, as it name implies, was white. The Sulphur was deep yellow and had an excellent flavour.

Blackcurrants were mostly Baldwin, raspberries Superlative, Raby Castel and Semper Fidelis and cherries River's Early, Black-heart and Morello.

Outdoor flowers, such as wallflowers, forget-me-nots and violets were grown for market. At one period Smith experimented with forcing lily of the valley for the Christmas market, using a glasshouse divided down the centre and one half darkened. 50,000 crowns of lily of the valley were planted in fish boxes, watered and placed on shelves. The darkened half of the house was kept at a high temperature and the other half at a moderate one. The 'valley' was forced in the darkened half, then brought out into the other half to get the leaves green before marketing. The experiment was such a success that in the following year five houses were used and 3,000,000 crowns. This, too, was a success from the cultivation point of view but Smith overreached himself on the marketing side. There were far too many to handle himself, so he made arrangements with six other market salesmen to sell on commission for him. The market became thoroughly glutted and by the end of the season Smith showed a loss of £500. He promptly turned the houses over to cucumbers.

Smith sold his own produce at Covent Garden on most days of the year. Each night, after a day's work and a few hours sleep, he would leave for the market, arriving about three o'clock in the morning. To conduct his business he sat at a portable desk which he brought with him from the farm.

Five or six pair-horse loads of produce would be sent up to the market of a night and while one wagon was being unloaded the others would wait in by-streets. Smith's customers included big departmental stores such as Harrods and the Army and Navy Stores. So his produce had to be top class. By five o'clock, most of the big buyers had come and gone and about seven o'clock in came the costermongers to bid for anything that might be left over.

Smith was fond of horses and his one relaxation was to attend sales, including Tattersalls, to buy them. At one time he had sixty horses—ponies, trap horses and cart horses—and they were always looked after with the greatest care. Every day the ration of oats and chaff and straw was carefully weighed out, bran mashes were given at regular periods, rock salt was provided and everything was spotlessly clean. The hours for the carters were five o'clock in the morning until seven at night. The first two hours of a morning for the carters were spent in feeding and cleaning the horses and at seven the horses left the stables to do a ten-hour day before they came home to be cleaned, fed, watered and bedded down for the night.

In fact, the horses seemed to have had a better life than the men. For digging ground, for example, the men were paid threepence a rod, unless the ground was extra heavy or under glass when they got fourpence. For digging between trees, where the space included that taken up by the trees, the pay was twopence halfpenny a rod. Hoeing brussels sprouts brought five shillings an acre : but this was only to hoe the part not done by the horse-hoe. Cauliflower under the same conditions merited sixpence. All these crops were hoed with a nine-inch hoe. For crops like spinach, beet and parsley, which were hoed with a six-inch hoe, the price was ten shillings an acre. Pickers were paid sixpence a half bushel for gooseberries, threepence halfpenny a peck for currants and a penny a pound for raspberries.

A great use was made of sacks as an article of clothing by the men. They would have them round their waist and, when wet, over their heads. Very few stopped work because of rain.

The dress of the women was almost uniform. They wore head handkerchiefs and a crochetted 'cross over' which came across each shoulder and was tied round the waist. Over this went a shawl, also tied round the waist but which could be discarded in hot weather. The skirt was long and could be pinned up. Under it they wore a coloured petticoat and over it a coarse apron which they changed to a white one when arriving or departing from the farm.

A. W. Smith died in 1927 from heart failure following a bout of influenza at the age of seventy-two. His main years were from 1890 to 1904. He set a standard, to quote his foreman Alfred Lucas, 'never passed by Englishman or foreigner. He raised the standard of English-grown produce to a height it had never reached before'.

APPENDIX

Where the Plants Came From

Most of the fruits, vegetables and flowers grown in the very early days of British horticulture were wild or semi-cultivated native plants. When traffic with the Continent became possible, new introductions started and as travel grew easier, so the range of plants grew.

Acquilegia see Columbine.

Almond *Amygdalus communis* is hardy enough to ripen its fruits in the south of England, though its real home is on the banks of the Mediterranean. Almonds were known to the Anglo-Saxons and have been grown in Britain since the sixteenth century, though almost entirely as an ornamental tree.

Amaryllis *Amaryllis belladonna* is the variety sold in shops. Known as Belladonna lily, it was introduced in the early eighteenth century. It has heads of large lily-like flowers on leafless stems.

Anemone *Anemone coronaria,* the poppy anemone, is the chief source of cultivated anemones, coming from southern Europe. There are two main types, the large single De Caen and the semi-double St Brigid. Mixed colours are usually marketed, though a few separate varieties are available. *Anemone fulgens,* with its narrow petals of brilliant scarlet, is sometimes seen. Known as Scarlet wind-flower, it also originates from southern Europe.

Apple The modern apple is of mixed breeding. The native crab *Malus communis* ssp *silvestris* and another wild apple *Malus communis pumila domestica* are involved, also the cherry apple or Siberian crab *M baccata* and many hybrids. It may have originated in the Black Sea area. It is grown on many types of trees ranging from tall standards to dwarf pyramids, using special root-stocks such as crab, M II and MM 106. Varieties are numerous but only a selected few are grown on a large scale commercially. Well known as dessert apples in Britain are Cox's Orange Pippin, Worcester Pearmain, Beauty of Bath, Miller's Seedling, James Grieve, Laxton's Superb and Ellison's Orange. Main cooking varieties are Early Victoria (syn Emneth Early), Grenadier, Lord Derby, Bramley's Seedling and Newton Wonder.

Apricot   *Prunus armeniaca.* Few are grown nowadays in Britain but in early days they featured as a luxury fruit in private hot houses. A relative of the peach and nectarine, it originated in warmer climes, probably, as its name implies, in Armenia.

Arbor-vita   This is the *Thuja* tree, introduced from America and the Far East in the late sixteenth century. Sometimes spelt Thuya, *T Lobbii* is often grown to provide foliage for use in wreaths.

Artichoke—globe   *Cynara scolymus.* No relation to the 'Jerusalem' and probably came from southern Europe. With the 'Jerusalem' the roots are eaten, with the 'globe' it is the flower-buds, the edible portion being the fleshy part of the bud scales which are green or purple and are boiled to make them soft.

Artichoke—Jerusalem   *Helianthus tuberosus,* the 'Jerusalem', is thought to be a corruption of the Italian 'gira sole', and so named because its flowers turn to follow the sun. But it came neither from Italy nor Israel, being a native of north America. There are red and white types but the white is not much grown in this country.

Asparagus   *Asparagus offininalis altilis* is the edible kind which originated in the temperate zone of the Old World but is native to many parts of Britain. There is little visual difference in the varieties: most have a purple tinge but all-white is popular on the Continent. The foliage of the edible asparagus is sold as asparagus tops for decoration but this must not be confused with *Asparagus plumosus nanus* (asparagus fern), *A asparagoides* (smilax) and *A sprengeri* (sprengeri) all of which are considerably used in the floral world.

Aspidistra	*Aspidistra elatior* (syn *A lurida*) is the common green type but a variety *variegata* has leaves striped cream. Introduced early in the nineteenth century from China, it became extremely popular during the Victorian era.
Aster	In the trade this is the China aster, *Callistephus*, of which there are many different types. They are used as cut flowers, pot plants and bedding plants. The main species is *C. chinensis* which, as its name implies, came originally from China. It was introduced to England in 1731.
Azalea	*Azalea indica* (botanically rhododendron) is the one grown most in pots. Known as the Indian azalea, it originated in China.
Balm	*Melissa officinalis* was introduced from southern Europe but is now native here. It was used to relieve headaches and as a wound dressing.
Balsam	*Impatiens balsamina* is the one grown outdoors in flower gardens during the summer.
Barberry	Can be either the coloured foliage of *Mahonia aquifolium* or the berried branches of many kinds of *Berberis*. The Mahonia probably came from the Himalayas and the others from various parts of China and Japan.
Bean	The scarlet runner bean, *Phaseolus multiflorus*, was introduced from South America in 1633 for the beauty of its brilliant red flowers. The French, or kidney bean, *Phaseolus vulgaris*, is another importation from South America and is of many different forms, eg stringless, green, waxpodded, bush, climbing, haricot and so on. The broad bean, *Vicia faba*, is no relation to the above, being of European origin. It is divided into Windsor and long-pod types but many varieties are now intermediate between the two.
Beetroot	*Beta vulgaris*, the common beetroot, stems from the wild sea beet, *Beta maritima*, which grows on British sea shores. From this source has been developed other types such as sugar beet and mangel wurzel. Beetroot can have round roots or long. They are often stored in clamps during the winter months.

Begonia A wide range of plants, some of which are grown for their flowers and others for their ornamental foliage. Introduced in the mid-eighteenth century.

Bittersweet *Solanum dulcamara.* This is the common woody nightshade with purple flowers and red berries that grows in hedges.

Borage *Borago officinalis* is a perennial herb first introduced from southern Europe but now naturalized in some places. Its leaves are used in pickles and salads and also added to alcoholic drinks. The flowers used to be candied and added to pot pourri.

Box *Buxus sempervirens* is used by florists as a background in wreaths and other designs. Also popular as a hedge plant, it is common to Europe, north and west Africa.

Broccoli This is correctly the sprouting broccoli, green and purple, which has a number of heads, as opposed to the cauliflower which has one. But the winter cauliflower is often called broccoli, especially in Cornwall. Sprouting broccoli is a descendant of the sea cabbage, *Brassica oleracea,* which grows on the coasts of England, Scotland and Wales.

Brussels sprout With the long botanical name of *Brassica oleracea bullata gemmifera*, the brussels sprout is one of many descendants of the wild cabbage. It has been known since the thirteenth century and possibly originated near Brussels, hence its name. Many varieties are available, varying in colour from light to dark green.

Buddleia Known as the butterfly bush, because the fragrant varieties are particularly attractive to butterflies, it was first introduced in the mid-eighteenth century, mostly from China.

Bullace *Prunus insititia.* A small wild plum and a relative of the wild hedgerow sloe.

Cabbage *Brassica oleracea capitata.* Originated from wild cabbage which grows on the shores of the Mediterranean, as well as in southern England. Can be divided into spring, summer, autumn

and winter types with many varieties of each
and the seasons overlap.

Camellia   *Camellia japonica.* The glossy green leaves are
used for decoration. Introduced early in the
eighteenth century from Japan. Also sold as a
flowering pot plant and cut flower.

Campion   *Lychnis alba* and some others grow wild in
Britain. There are many other types, some of
which are known under names such as melan-
drium, viscaria and agrostemma. The one sold
in the early days was probably the native white
campion, ragged robin or red campion.

Carnation   The perpetual flowering carnation, the one
grown commercially under glass, is of mixed
parentage from various species of *Dianthus.* It
is quite distinct from the clove picotee and border
carnation which derive from *D caryophyllus.*
The perpetual flowering is believed to have
originated in France about 1750, when it was
known as the mayonnais and the de Mahon.

Cauliflower   *Brassica oleracea botrytis.* The cauliflower is
simply a cabbage that develops its flower buds
into one large curd. The true cauliflower is hardy
only out of doors in the summer but otherwise
closely resembles the broccoli or winter cauliflower. Its exact origin is unknown but it has
been grown in Britain for several hundreds of
years.

Celery   *Apium graveolens.* Wild celery or smallage is
common in ditches and marshy places in the
lowlands. Two main types: ordinary, which is
earthed up to blanch the leaf stalks, and self-
blanching which does not need this treatment.

Cherry   Two forms, *Prunus avium,* the sweet cherry, and
P cerasus the morello. *P avium* is derived from
wild forms that are widespread in western Asia
and Europe while *P cerasus* is a native of the
Middle East. Neither was taken under cultivation until historical times. There are three wild
cherries in Britain: the bird, gean and bitter.
Cultivated cherries can be divided into bigarreau
(two-coloured, firm flesh), gean (sweet) and duke
(hybrid between sweet and acid) and acid. Many

named sweet varieties such as Early Rivers, Roundel Heart, Waterloo, Gaucher, Noble, Amber, Napoleon Bigarreau and Turkey Heart are grown in England.

Cherry bay This could be the bay laurel (*Laurus nobilis*) used to crown the Roman victors, or the cherry laurel (*Prunus laurocerasus*).

Chervil *Anthriscus cerefolium*, a white-flowered annual sometimes found growing wild as an escape from cultivation. Its leaves are used to season dishes. First introduced in the mid-seventeenth century.

Chestnut *Castanea sativa* rarely ripens its fruits north of the Midlands. Although native, it is scarce as a wild tree. Probably introduced by the Romans.

Chrysanthemum The florist's chrysanthemum is botanically known as *Chrysanthemum sinense* or *C morifolium* and is probably a hybrid form that was obtained, centuries ago, as a result of hybridization between *C indicum*, the Chinese chrysanthemum, and other species. A century or more ago the plant was commonly referred to as *C indicum*. Probably originated in the Far East.

Chicory *Cichorium intybus* grows wild in England and can be used for salads and medicine and as a substitute for coffee. Commonest garden form is the Dutch witloof, or white-leaf chicory.

Chives *Allium schoenoprasum* is native but rare, occurring along stream-sides in Cornwall and Northumberland. It is common to north Asia and has an onion odour.

Cineraria *Senecio cruentus*, of which the most popular varieties are best known as *Cineraria grandiflora* and *C multiflora*. Introduced in the early eighteenth century and probably originated in the Canary Isles.

Cinquefoil Probabaly the marsh cinquefoil, *Comarum palustre*, which bears conspicuous purple blossoms in June.

Coleus These ornamental leaved plants came from the Far East in the mid-eighteenth century.

Columbine *Aquilegia vulgaris*. This is native to England but has been cultivated in gardens as long as records exist. The name occurs in a poem in 1310 and both Chaucer and Shakespeare were familiar with it. The modern long-stemmed hybrids are derived from *A coerula* which came from the Rocky Mountains in 1864 or *A chrysantha* introduced from California in 1873.

Cowberry
: *Vaccinium vitis-idaea* is wild in parts of Britain and has bright red berries that are made into a jelly resembling cranberry jelly.

Cornflower
: *Cynaus minor* is a native of Britain in its deep blue form. Also grown now in white and pink.

Cowslip
: *Primula veris* (see primrose). Special forms of cowslip were cultivated in gardens from earliest days.

Cuckoo flower
: *Cardamine pratensis,* or the meadow cress, whose leaves can be used as a salad but have a bitter taste.

Cucumber
: *Cucumis sativus.* A wild cucumber, *C sativus hardwickii,* is considered to be the progenitor of the cultivated cucumber. It has from time immemorial been cultivated in India and from there it went to Egypt and later via the Romans to Europe and England. Two main types, ridge and ordinary.

Currant
: Black, red and white. The black, *Ribes nigrum* and the red, *R rubrum* both grow wild throughout much of Britain and although their names are derived from the true grape currants of Corinth, both are native shrubs. Cultivated varieties are not more than 500 years old. White, *R sylvestre album* is an albino strain of the red. Varieties in Britain are numerous and include (black) Baldwin, Wellington, Blacksmith, Boskoop Giant and Amos Black; (red) Red Lake, Fay's Prolific and Laxton's Perfection; (white) White Versailles, White Pearl and White Dutch.

Cyclamen
: *Cyclamen persicum* has many varieties and strains. It was mentioned as a new or rare plant in 1651. Came to this country via Greece and Syria.

Dahlia
: Many types and varieties, originating mostly from *Dahlia pinnata,* a native of Mexico where

it was probably grown in Aztec times. Said to have first flowered in England at Holland House, Kensington, in the seventeenth century.

Damson A variety of *Prunus domestica*. Botanists sometimes put the damson in the *P insititia* or bullace group but the damsons now cultivated in Britain have their origin in varieties imported many hundreds of years ago from Damascus where they have been grown since before the Christian era. Damson is a shortened form of Damascene. Named varieties in England include Farleigh, Merryweather and Shropshire.

Dandelion *Taraxacum officinale* was once popular in salads. It needs to be blanched to be used in this way. Native to Britain.

Daphne Many species cultivated but the fragrant *D mezereum,* the old mezereon, is well known with its purplish-red or white flowers in February and March. Probably originated in Siberia.

Dogwood Common name for the range of trees and shrubs of the *Cornus* family. It is noted for its coloured leaves.

Doronicum A pure yellow, daisy-like flower sometimes called leopard's bane. *Doronicum plantagineum* from Europe is the variety most grown.

Dragon's tongue Probably *Dracocephalum moldavica,* a herb introduced from Siberia in the late sixteenth century and often referred to as 'Dragon's head'.

Evening primrose *Oenothera biennis* from North America. A yellow fragrant flower.

Fennel *Foeniculum vulgare* is a native plant mainly on waste lands near the coast. Has been grown since Roman times as a pot herb and garnish and is used in salads. There are several cultivated varieties but finnochio *F azoricum* is a distinct plant with a celery-like flavour as opposed to the aniseed flavour of our native fennel.

Feverfew *Chrysanthemum parthenium,* or bachelor's button, grows in the hedgerows. It gets its name from the claim that it can cure fevers as well as relieving coughs and the pain of insect bites.

Fig	*Ficus carica.* Has been grown in the south of England since the sixteenth century but is a native of the Mediterranean. This is the hardy species of fig.
Filbert	*Corylus maxima* is very similar to the cob-nut or *C avellana*. The filbert is entirely covered by the husk, but the cob is not. They are both cultivated varieties of the native hazel. Found in temperate zones throughout the world.
Fritillary	*Fritillaria imperialis* is the crown imperial, a native of Persia, introduced to Britain in the sixteenth century. There is also a native fritillary, the snake's head or chequered daffodil, *F meleagris*, and a white *alba*.
Fuchsia	Many varieties. Mostly introductions from South America, where it originated. Came to Britain towards the end of the eighteenth century.
Gardenia	The *Gardenia florida intermedia* and the *G grandiflora* are the two varieties grown for market and which were most popular in Victorian and Edwardian days. The *grandiflora* came from Cochin-China in the mid-eighteenth century but the origin of the *intermedia* is unknown.
Garlic	The true garlic, *Allium sativum*, is rarely grown in Britain but the native field garlic, *A oleraceum*, is sometimes gathered as a seasoning. There are several other native wild garlics.
Genista	The native genista gave its name to the English kings, the Plantagenets, whose badge was the *planta genista*. The petty whin, *Genista anglica*, is common on the heaths of the New Forest.
Geranium	The Geranium, or *Pelargonium zonale*, has been a popular window box and pot plant for over 100 years. The ivy-leaved geranium (*Pelargonium peltatum*) was in great demand in Edwardian days. Both originated in South Africa. The real geranium, the cranesbill family, is native to Britain in several varieties.
Gillyflower	The clove carnation, supposed to have been discovered in Spain in the time of Augustus Caesar, was often known by this name. The Spaniards used it to give a spicy flavour to beverages which

M

gave the clove carnation another name of 'sops-in-wine'. The wallflower was also known as the yellow stock gillyflower. And stocks themselves were often called stock gillyflowers.

Gladiolus

The native gladiolus is *Gladiolus illyricus* but it is rare. Many European species, however, were imported as early as the sixteenth century. There are three main groups in florist's gladioli—early-flowering *colvillei* and *nanus*; large-flowered; and *primulinus* hybrids.

Golden rod

Solidago virgaurea. The common golden rod comes from Europe but species from North America have been introduced. It is used as a yellow spray or background flower.

Gooseberry

Ribes grossularia. Originated in Europe and North Africa and reached Britain in the sixteenth century. But only five varieties were known by the eighteenth century. Became very popular as a show fruit. Well-known varieties are Leveller, Lancashire Lad, Whinham's Industry, Keepsake, Careless and May Duke.

Grape

The grape-bearing vine, *Vitis vinifera*, has been cultivated in Britain since its introduction, probably by monks, early in the middle ages. It is hardy in the south of England. This particular vine probably originated in the Caucasian region. Not many are cultivated in glasshouses now. Main varieties are Cannon Hall, Black Hamburgh, Gros Colmar, Muscat of Alexandria and Alicante.

Ground ivy

The leaves of this *Glechoma hederacea* were formerly dried to make herb tea.

Hazel nut

(see Filbert)

Heartsease

A member of the pansy family, the heartsease, or *Viola tricolor*, is one of the parents of the modern pansy.

Heath

The principal heathers grown as pot plants are *Erica gracilis*, *E nivalis* and *E hyemalis*. Many wild heathers exist and would have been gathered for sale in early days. Most heathers are a form of *Erica*, but ling heather is *Calluna vulgaris*.

Hollyhock

Althea rosea was introduced from China sometime during the middle of the sixteenth century.

Althea officinalis is the marsh mallow native to Britain.

Honeysuckle   There are many forms of *Lonicera*, ranging from the common weed to species introduced from the Far East.

Horehound   *Marrubium vulgare* is gathered for herb teas and beers and still has a reputation as a cough cure. It is a native.

Hurtleberry   (see Whortleberry)

Hyacinth   *Hyacinthus orientalis* is the main type grown as a pot plant. It was introduced in the late sixteenth century from the Mediterranean area.

Hydrangea   Another early eighteenth century introduction. The pot plant mostly used is *Hydrangea macrophylla*, of which there are hundreds of varieties. It originally came from China and Japan.

Hyssop   This dwarf evergreen shrub, *Hyssopus officinalis*, derives its name from the Hebrew *azob*, or holy herb. It came to Britain from the Mediterranean and though now used as an edging plant, was formerly in favour as a pungent herb.

Indiarubber plant   The *Ficus elastica* which originated in India is a member of the fig family.

Iris   There are two native iris, the gladdon, *Iris foetidissima*, and the sweet flag, *I pseudacorus*. Sweet flag is the *fleur de lys* of heraldry and was used for medicine and as a dye. Cultivated iris have been introduced from many parts of the world and there are a large number of varieties.

Ixia   This is the African corn lily of several species. It came to Britain in the early eighteenth century.

Kale   Kale is a descendant of the wild cabbage, *Brassica oleracea*. Kales were formerly a common crop in Scotland. Some kales are used as a winter feed for sheep and cattle.

Laburnum   *Laburnum alpinum*, the Scottish laburnum and *L anagyroides* (syn *vulgare*), the golden chain, both came from Europe in the late sixteenth century. There are many varieties.

Larkspur

This is the annual form of delphinium. The blue, white or rose *Delphinium ajacio* (syn *D gayanum*) is known as the rocket larkspur, while *D consolida* has taller branches and is mainly blue. But many varieties in other shades have been developed from these. The annuals are a European introduction.

Lavender

Lavendula vera is a native of the Mediterranean but the English strain is the one most esteemed. First introduced in the mid-sixteenth century. Used for making perfume and, in years gone by, in particular for filling sachets or making pot pourri.

Leek

Allium porrum. This is descended, in part at least, from the wild leek, *Allium ampeloprasum*, which is found near the sea. Its origin is uncertain but may have been Switzerland.

Lemon

The various citruses with their edible fruits came to Britain in the sixteenth century and proved very popular with the nobility and rich people. *Citrus limonia*, the lemon, came from Asia.

Lettuce

Lactuca sativa. Originated in India or Central Asia but four wild species occur locally in Britain on walls, shingle banks and waste places and were, no doubt, once gathered to eat. Several forms, such as cabbage, cos and salad, have been evolved and there are countless varieties of these.

Lilac

Syringa vulgaris, the fragrant common lilac, originated from eastern Europe and came to Britain somewhere at the beginning of the sixteenth century. Many other species, mainly from the Far East, have been introduced since.

Lily

These cover a wide range but those which have been grown most, commercially, are the *Lilium longiflorum* (Easter lily), *L auratum* (golden-rayed), *L rubrum* (Turk's cap), *L candidum* (madonna), *L tigrinum* (tiger). Some are specially forced in glasshouses, others are grown out of doors. Lilies are one of our oldest introductions, the first probably arriving in the middle ages before 1400. *L candidum* was in existence 3,000 years ago.

Lily of the valley	*Convallaria majallis* is a native of Britain and grows wild in many parts. The large florist lily of the valley is grown from specially-treated crowns bought mainly from Germany.
Lupin	*Lupinus polyphyllus* is the lupin from which most of the varieties seen in the florists' shops have been developed. It came from California. The first lupins were introduced from North America in the late sixteenth century.
Madder	The wide madder, *Rubia peregrina*, occurs naturally in the south and west of England. The cultivated form, *R tinctorum*, was at one time grown in England as a vegetable dye.
Maidenhair fern	Species of *Adiantum* are grown as pot plants or for foliage. *A decorum* is the main type grown for cutting.
Mangold or Mangel wurzel	A German 'famine root' which thrives under difficult conditions. Grown almost entirely for stock feeding and valued for its high sugar content.
Marigold	*Calendula officinalis*, the pot or Scotch marigold, is the most common variety, though the African marigold, *Tagetes erecta*, is to be found in shops during the summer months. The *Calendula* came from south Europe, the *Tagetes,* despite its name, from Mexico in the late sixteenth century.
Marjoram	Wild marjoram, *Origanum vulgare*, is confined to chalk and limestone soils. It was once used to flavour ale and the flowering tops served as a dye. Other varieties grown as herbs are sweet marjoram, *O marjorana*; perennial marjoram, *O onites*; and winter marjoram, *O peracleoticum*, all natives of the Mediterranean. As herbs, they are used to flavour salads and soups or to make herb tea.
Medlar	One of the oldest British fruits, the *Mespilus germanica* originated in Europe and Asia Minor and is still gathered for sale in small quantities. The fruit needs to be allowed to get overripe (bletted) before eating.
Melon	The melon, *Cucumis melo*, is of tropical or subtropical origin and has been cultivated in eastern

and Mediterranean lands since Biblical times. Two main types in Britain are: netted and canteloupe. Netted are so called from the lace pattern on the skin, canteloupe after Cantelupa in Italy where it was introduced from Armenia in the fifteenth century. Other varieties are charentais, ogen and tiger.

Mezereon   (see Daphne)

Michaelmas daisy   Innumerable varieties of this *Aster* exist, including *amellus, cordifolius, diffusus, ericoides, novae belgii and novae angliae*. They come from many parts of the world. One from North America was named after Tradescant in 1637. The original starwort came from Italy about 1596.

Mignonette   The *Reseda odorata*, once one of the most popular of pot plants, is now little heard of except in old-fashioned gardens. It is grown commercially for its perfume in the south of France, where it is native. It was probably brought to England in the mid-eighteenth century from North Africa or Egypt.

Mint   The type of mint most used for culinary purposes is the spearmint, or *Mentha spicata*. This was originally introduced from the Mediterranean but is now naturalised in Britain. Peppermint, *M piperita*, is also native to Britain.

Mugwort   *Artemisia vulgaris* is very similar to wormwood (which see) but less aromatic.

Mulberry   The presence in England of the mulberry (*Morus nigra*) is largely due to King James I who imported large numbers about 1609 to provide food for silkworms. It is a native of Asia Minor. The fruit resembles a raspberry and wine can be made from it.

Mushroom   *Psalliota (Agaricus) campestris* is the wild mushroom and is widespread. The cultivated variety has no true botanical name but *P hortensis* or *P bispora* are used.

Musk   *Mimulus moschatus*, a little yellow-flowered pot plant, was introduced from North America in the nineteenth century but the true strain seems to have been lost and few plants now have the original fragrance.

Mustard	White mustard, *Sinapis alba*, used to be mixed with cress to make mustard and cress. Now rape, *Brassica napus*, is often used on its own. Mustard can also be used as sheep fodder or for ploughing in.
Myrtle	The common myrtle, *(Myrtus bullata* syn *M communis)*, came from West Africa. Other species came from New Zealand and Chile.
Narcissus	The daffodil, *Narcissus pseudo-narcissus*, is a native. Two other narcissi, *N biflorus*, the jonquil, and *N poeticus*, the pheasant's eye, are well established in the south-west of England, though doubtful natives. Daffodil bulbs were once used as an emetic. Most cultivated species are from Europe, though a few are from the Far East.
Nectarine	*Prunus nectarina* originated in China or Persia, probably as a sport from a peach tree. The fruit differs from a peach in having a smooth skin, firmer flesh and a richer glow of colour. Well-known varieties are John Rivers, Elruge, Humboldt, Lord Napier and Pineapple.
Nephros	Ferns of the *Nephrolepis* family, introduced from tropical regions in late eighteenth century.
Oleander	*Nerium oleander*, the oleander or rose bay, comes from the Orient and was introduced to Britain in the late sixteenth century.
Onion	The genus *Allium* includes onions, leeks and garlic. The common garden onion is derived from the wild *A cepa*, a native of western Asia. It was grown by the ancient Egyptians. Various strains of onions are grown for different purposes : spring onions are gathered immature to be eaten raw, many are grown for their bulbs. Spanish is the name given to any large mild variety.
Orange	*Citrus sinensis* is the common, or sweet, orange which came originally from China. Introduced to Britain in the sixteenth century.
Orchid	Orchids used by florists are mostly cattleyas, cymbidiums, cypripediums and odontoglossums. The cattleya comes from South America, the cymbidium from India, Burma, Assam and

neighbouring countries, the cypripedium from both hemispheres and the odontoglosssum from South America.

Palm

Large palms, either *Howea (Kentia) forsteriana* and *H (Kentia) belmoreana*, were in Victorian times much in demand for society weddings and public functions. Both these species came from Lord Howe's Island in the Tasman Sea.

Pampas grass

Cortaderia selloana (syn *C argentea*) is grown for its silky silver plumes which can be dried and used for winter decoration. It was introduced from the Argentine, probably in the sixteenth century.

Pansy

Viola lutea, the mountain pansy, grows in the Pennines. *V tricolor*, the heartsease, is one of the parents of the modern pansy but cultivated species have been obtained from many parts of the world.

Parsley

Carum petroselinum is not a native plant but reached us in the sixteenth century or earlier from the Mediterranean, where it was cultivated in classical times as *petroselinum* by both Greeks and Romans.

Parsnip

Pastinaca sativa is a native plant that has been brought into cultivation.

Passion flower

This is the *Passiflora* family which came to Britain early seventeenth century from central and south America. Two species produce edible fruits.

Pea

Pisum sativum hortense originated from the Mediterranean area. The native British pea is *Lathyrus maritimus*, which bears an edible though bitter seed. The field pea, the *Pisum arvense*, has hard brown seeds when ripe. There are several types of garden pea such as blue round, marrowfat and sugar peas (mangetout) and many named varieties.

Peach

The *Prunus persica* originated in China and was possibly brought to Britain by the Romans, though it is not heard of as growing in this country until the late sixteenth century. Some varieties have 'free' stones; other 'cling' stones. Well-known varieties are : Duke of York, Hale's Early, Peregrine and Royal George.

Pear

The wild pear, *Pyrus communis*, is a tall tree of woods and hedgerows. Its fruit is woody and not worth eating. Varieties brought in from the Continent have chiefly been responsible for the developing English dessert, cooking and perry pears. Perry pears are grown mostly in the West Country. Dessert varieties include Dr Jules Guyot, William's Bon Chrétien, Conference and Doyenné du Comice. Pears are mostly grown on quince or pear rootstocks.

Pelargonium

(see Geranium)

Pennyroyal

This is one of the mint family and, besides being cultivated in gardens, grows wild along the sides of streams. Its botanical name is *Mentha pulegium*.

Phlox

The phlox family was not introduced to Britain until the early eighteenth century, when they were brought from North America.

Pink

Dianthus plumarius, the cottage pink, is native to Britain and eastern Europe. Cultivated species came from many parts of the world including Siberia. Its cultivation goes back to the time of the Cistercian monks.

Plum

Prunus domestica except damson, *P insititia*, and cherry plum, *P cerasifera*. The modern plum is a development of the wild hedgerow sloe and the bullace, but in its present form probably originated in the Caucasus. It is grown on special rootstocks. A few well-known varieties are Czar, Pershore, Victoria, Warwickshire Drooper, Marjorie's Seedling, Monarch and Pond's Seedling. Gages are small, round green plums, with names such as Greengage, Oullin's Golden Gage and Jefferson.

Poppy

The Iceland poppy, *Papaver nudicaule*, is the most common poppy grown to sell. It came from the Arctic regions. The corn poppy, *P rhoeas*, is the one found in cornfields, or *P somniferum*, the opium poppy.

Pomegranate	*Punica granatum* was introduced from Persia and Afghanistan in the mid-sixteenth century. Seldom produces fruit in Britain.
Potato	The wild *Solanum tuberosum* came from three centres in South America—Mexico, Bolivian and Peruvian Andes and Chïloé Island. From the few forms that were imported into Europe at the end of the sixteenth century, and then again in the nineteenth century, have evolved the many varieties of today. Two main varieties used commercially at the present time are King Edward VII and Majestic.
Primrose	(see Primula)
Primula	There is a small wild primula, the bird's eye primrose, *Primula farinosa*. Also the oxlip, *P elatior*; the polyanthus, *P polyantha*; the cowslip, *P veris*, and the primrose *P vulgaris*. But greenhouse species are from many countries and first introductions were made at the end of the sixteenth century.
Pteris	Large genus of mainly tropical ferns.
Pumpkin	The pumpkin is a member of the *Cucurbita* and has watery fruits that reach a very large size. *Cucurbita moschata*, the pumpkin, is of unknown origin and came to Britain in the late sixteenth century.
Quince	The *Cydonia vulgaris*, though long known in Britain, is an alien tree coming from Persia and finding its way to Europe via Greece. It is the golden apple of ancient times and emblem of love and happiness. Varieties include appleshaped, pear-shaped and Portugal. It was introduced to Britain about the sixteenth century.
Radish	Wild radish, *Raphanus raphanistrum*, occurs as a weed in Britain. The main stock of the garden radish is considered to be the Oriental species, *R sativus*, which came from southern Asia some time in the middle of the sixteenth century. There is also a long rooted radish, *R longipinnatus*, known as the China radish, which is sometimes cultivated.
Ranunculus	The cultivated ranunculus was very popular at the end of the nineteenth century. There are

three distinct groups : *Ranunculus asiaticus superbissimus,* the French ranunculus; *R a vulgaris,* the Persian and Turban types; and *R a sanguineus,* the Turkey or paeony and the one grown commercially as a cut flower. These are all tuberous-rooted species.

Rape

Brassica napus, the rape, is the main constituent nowadays of the familiar domestic mustard and cress. Rape can be found growing wild. Farmers use it as sheep fodder or for ploughing in as green manure.

Raspberry

Rubus idaes originated in the temperate parts of Africa, Asia and America. The wild raspberry grows in the Scottish forests and to a lesser extent further south. The old Scots name for raspberry was hindberry. The cultivated raspberry is extensively grown in eastern Scotland and in Kent, Worcestershire and East Anglia.

Rhododendron

A large shrub family of which *Rhododendron ponticum,* the parent of most hardy kinds, was introduced to Britain in the mid-eighteenth century. Flowering branches of rhododendron are used by florists when any form that carries its blossom well and is brightly coloured is suitable.

Rhubarb

Rheum rhaponticum comes from central Asia and was not introduced to Europe until the eighteenth century. The wild rhubarb, *Rumex alpinus,* or monk's rhubarb, is not a true rhubarb. Cultivated rhubarb is grown from crowns and either forced in special sheds or grown as an outdoor crop. It became popular in the mid-nineteenth century first as 'physic' and then as a useful 'sweet'.

Rose

The rose family includes several that are native to Britain, *Rosa canina,* the dog rose, being the best known. Most of the roses now sold by florists are of the hybrid tea type which came from China. But popular many years ago were the moss, cabbage, damask, York and Lancaster, musk, and many others. Dwarf polyantha and rambler roses are sold in pots.

Rosemary

Rosmarinus officinalis is one of our most fragrant shrubs, though it is not used now as a seasoning for meat. In Saxon times, its fragrance was employed to blot out less desirable smells. Its oil is employed in medicine and widely used in perfumery. Rosemary is a recognised symbol of remembrance and sprigs are in demand at times like Armistice Day.

Rue

Ruta graveolens from the Mediterranean was used in salads, for flavouring drinks and for strewing rooms 'to ward off the plague'.

Saffron

The saffron that gave its name to Saffron Walden in Essex was *Crocus sativus*. The name comes from the Arabic *zaffer* and it is a native of Persia. The cultivation of saffron to be used as a dye became a considerable industry. It was also used for colouring butter and in cooking.

Sage

Salvia officinalis was brought to Britain from the Mediterranean zone during the Middle Ages. Its name is derived from the Latin *salvere*, to save—a tribute to its healing properties. It does not grow wild in Britain.

Salsify

Tragopogon porrifolius is grown for its succulent roots and its often called the vegetable oyster. Probably came from America or southern Europe. A doubtful native of Britain.

Sassafras

An aromatic tree, *S albidum* (syn *S officinale*), from north-eastern America.

Savoy

Brassica oleracea bullata major originated from the wild cabbage and was introduced from Savoy probably in the seventeenth century. The savoy is distinguished by its peculiar corrugated foliage with outstanding veins.

Scabious

The sky-blue devil's bit, *Scabiosa succisa*, is a native of our chalk downs but the perennial *Scabiosa caucasica* grown commercially is, as its name suggests, from the Caucasus.

Scurvy grass

Takes its name from its use by sailors as a medicine to prevent or cure scurvy. It is of the genus *Cochlearia*, little cress-like white-flowered plants of the seashore. *C officinalis* is the variety which was cultivated and used in salads.

Seakale	*Crambe maritima* grows wild on the sea coasts of western Europe and on the southern shores of England. Under cultivation, the roots are forced and blanched. Popular in the last century but little cultivated now.
Shallot	*Allium ascalonicum* is a native of Palestine and its name is said to be a corruption of Askkelon. The small bulbs, or shallots, are used mainly for pickling. It has been in cultivation for many hundreds of years.
Skirret	This is an edible, carrot-like root of the *Sium sisarum*, which is seldom cultivated these days, though it was introduced from east Asia in the mid-sixteenth century. The root has a strange taste.
Snapdragon	*Antirrhinum majus* is known also as calves' snout and lion's mouth. Comes from southern Europe but it is not known who introduced it. It is naturalised in Britain. Cultivated out of doors and under glass.
Snowdrop	The native snowdrop is *Galanthus nivalis* and is still mainly grown in the wild state and picked for sale, as it has been for several hundreds of years. Other varieties come from both Europe and Asia Minor.
Solanum	*Solanum capsicastrum*, the winter cherry, and *S pseudocapsicum*, the Jerusalem cherry, are popular pot plants, particularly around Christmas time. They came originally from South America.
Sorrel	Two types of sorrel, common, *Rumex acetosa*; and sheep's, *R acetosella*, are edible. In France it is cultivated in permanent beds and marketed under the name of oseille. *R patientia* is sometimes used as a substitute for spinach.
Southernwood	*Artemisia abrotanum*, known as lad's love or old man, is now only grown in cottage gardens for its fragrance.
Spinach	*Spinacea oleracea* originated in the far East and came to England about the mid-sixteenth century. It is of two cultivated types : round-seeded (summer) and prickly-seeded (winter). There is

also New Zealand spinach *(Terragonia expansa)* and spinach beet *(Beta vulgaris cicla)*.

Spiraea

Spiraea ulmaria is the wild meadowsweet while *S filipendula* is the dropwort. The roots of both there were at one time roasted for food. Meadowsweet was used to strew rooms in order to perfume the air, and has also been used as a substitute for tea. Other species of spiraea are flowering shrubs.

Stock

Mathiola was introduced early in the eighteenth century from southern Europe and became very popular. The ones used by florists were formerly divided into the annual ten-week stocks and the biennial Brompton stocks, with the East Lothian as a subsidiary group. But so much hybridization has been carried out in recent years that classification is now difficult.

Strawberry

The common wild strawberry, *Fragaria vesca*, was grown in French gardens in the fourteenth century : it was occasionally joined by the alpine, *F viridis*. But not until the scarlet Virginia strawberry, *F virginiana*, and the large Chilean, *F chiloensis*, were hybridized in Holland in the mid-eighteenth century did the modern strawberry, *F grandiflora*, emerge. Modern varieties change with the years. Those now grown commercially in Britain include Cambridge Favourite, Royal Sovereign, Redgauntlet, Talisman, Templar and Crusader.

Swede

The swede or swedish turnip, *Brassica campestris rutabaga*, is distinguished from the common turnip by smoother foliage and a 'neck' between root and leaves. The two main types are : bronze top and purple top. It has been cultivated in Britain for hundreds of years and originated from the field brassica, a plant closely allied to the wild turnip.

Sweet pea

Although sweet peas, *Lathyrus odoratus*, are popularly thought of as an outdoor summer flower, they are also grown under glass for sale in the spring. They were introduced from Italy early in the eighteenth century.

Sweet potato	*Impomoea batatas* is the tropical sweet potato with its edible tubers. It is not grown much in this country, but quite large supplies are imported to cater for immigrants.
Sweet William	This old-fashioned flower is *Dianthus barbatus* and came from southern Europe. Two main types : show, with smooth-edged petals with dark centres; and auricula-eyed, smooth-edged petals with white eye, surrounded by crimson or other tints.
Thyme	*Thymus vulgaris* originated in the Mediterranean. There are several varieties, their main difference being in the size of the leaf, though the lemon thyme has a distinctive lemon flavour. A wild thyme, *T serpyllum*, can be found mainly on chalk downs. Thyme is used as a kitchen herb either fresh or dried.
Tobacco	*Nicotiana tabacum* is the species grown considerably by the tobacco industry. It is hardy enough to ripen in Britain. The name *Nicotiana* commemorates Jean Nicot, who introduced tobacco to France in 1559. The central American Indians had been smoking tobacco for centuries before Columbus visited the country in 1492. *Nicotiana rustica* was the variety most grown in Britain in the seventeenth century.
Tomato	*Lycopersicon esculentum* originated in South America, west of the Andes. Other types of tomato such as the cherry, pear, and currant exist. It came to Britain as long ago as the sixteenth century but until the nineteenth century was grown for decoration only. It is grown indoors and out, and varieties are changing all the time. Favourites in recent years in Britain have been Ailsa Craig, Potentate, Moneymaker and Eurocross.
Tradescantia	The spiderwort and the wandering jew, both named after John Tradescant in the early seventeenth century.
Tulip	The tulip, *Tulipa*, which came to England in the late sixteenth century is of many species but the ones used in commerce may be divided into

early singles, early doubles, mendels, triumphs, darwin and cottage. For cut blooms, the darwins are the most used. Tulips can be grown out of doors or forced under glass. It was first cultivated as a garden flower in Turkey at the beginning of the sixteenth century.

Turnip

Brassica napus probably originated from the wild turnip in Europe or western Europe. In Anglo-Saxon times, the turnip was called *nepa*, but it was not until the early eighteenth century that they were used on a large scale to provide winter feed for sheep and cattle. Selected varieties are used as a table vegetable. They vary in shape and colour of flesh.

Verbena

Introduced from South America in the mid-eighteenth century and mainly used for bedding plants.

Violet

The wood violet, *Viola sylvestris*, grows wild in most parts of Europe, including Britain. Others to be found are *V canina*, the dog violet; *V calcarata* the spurred violet; *V lutea*, the mountain violet; *V odorata*, the sweet violet; and *V palustris*, the marsh violet. Varieties sold by florists are large types of *V odorata* and can be scented like Princess of Wales or unscented like Governor Herrick. Parma violets were once popular but are not very hardy and seldom grown now in Britain. The sweet violet has probably been cultivated in Britain since gardens began.

Virginia stock

Malcomia maritima has been in Britain since the early eighteenth century, having originated in southern Europe.

Wallflower

The *Cheirianthus cheiri* is a very old-established flower in Britain. It was often known as gillyflower, though clove carnations and stocks sometimes received this name also. The wallflower may be a true native of Britain or have been brought over at the time of the Norman Conquest.

Walnut

Juglans regia comes from Asia Minor but has been growing in Britain since the sixteenth century, more for its nuts than its timber. The walnuts are either picked while the shells are soft for pickling, or harvested ripe in September or October.

Watercress *Nasturtium officinale* grows wild along the banks of many a stream in Britain and differs very little from the cultivated forms which are grown on a vast scale today. Mostly green types are grown but a brown was at one time popular.

Winter savory *Satureia montana*, a shrubby perennial from the Mediterranean area, was once used extensively for seasoning. The summer savory, *S hortensis*, is an annual and is also used for flavouring.

Wormwood This unattractive native weed, *Artemisia absinthium*, derives its name from its use in olden days as a cure for internal worms.

Whortleberry *Vaccinium myrtillus*, the whortleberry, which grows wild on hills such as the Quantocks, is known in other parts of the country as wimberry, whinberry, huckleberry, bilberry, blaeberry, wort or hurt. Its berries ripen from green to black in August and are baked in tarts or made into jam.

Zinnia This South American flower came to Britain in the mid-eighteenth century. It can be grown out of doors or under glass. There is a range of types from the giant to the lilliput.

N

BIBLIOGRAPHY

CHAPTER ONE

Although plenty of books have been written on the history of gardening, they deal mainly with famous gardens and the men who designed them or had them in their charge. For the men who served horticulture in a more commercial way, it is necessary to extract information from many sources. The following will help.

AMHERST, ALICIA (afterwards Lady E. Cecil). *A History of Gardening in England*, 3rd Ed, 1910

BENNETT, L. G. *The Horticultural Industry of Middlesex*. University of Reading, 1952

BRADLEY, R. *A Survey of the Ancient Husbandry and Gardening*, Motte, 1725

CLAPHAM, J. H. *Concise Economic History of England to 1750*, Cambridge U. P, 1949

CLIFFORD, DEREK. *A History of Garden Design*, Faber & Faber, 1962

COX, E. H. M. *A History of Gardening in Scotland*, Chatto and Windus, 1935

CRISP, FRANK. *Medieval Gardens*, 2 vols, Lane, 1924

DRUMMOND, J. C. and WILLBRAHAM, A. *The Englishman's Food*, Cape, 1959

DUTTON, R. *The English Garden*, Batsford, 2nd Ed, 1950

ERNLE, R. E. *English Farming Past and Present*, Longmans, 6th Ed, 1961

FAIRBROTHER, NAN. *Men and Gardens*, Hogarth, 1956

FINSBERG, H. P. R. *The Agrarian History of England & Wales*, Cambridge U. P, 1967

FITTER, R. S. R. *London's Natural History*, Collins, 1945

FOOT, P. *General View of the Agriculture of the County of Middlesex*, John Nichols, 1794

FURNIVAL, F. J. *Harrison's Description of England in Shakespeare's Youth*, 1877

HADFIELD, MILES. *Gardening in Britain*, Hutchinson, 1960

HAZLITT, W. C. *Gleanings in Old Garden Literature*, Stock, 1889

HOSKINS, W. G. *Local History in England*, Longmans, 1959

HYAMS, E. and JACKSON, A. A. *The Orchard and Fruit Garden*, Longmans, 1961

JOHNSON, G. W. *A History of English Gardening*, Baldwin and Cradock, 1829

LOUDON, J. C. *An Encyclopedia of Gardening*, Longmans, 1834

MIDDLETON, JOHN. *General View of the Agriculture of Middlesex*, 1790

MILLER, P. *The Gardener's and Florist's Dictionary*, Rivington, 1724

NUSSEY, H. G. *London Gardens of the Past*, Lane, 1939

PHILLIPS, HENRY. *Pomarium Britannicum*, Allman, 1820

ROGERS, THOROLD. *Six Centuries of Work and Wages*, Allen and Unwin, 1884

SEEBOHM, M. E. *The Evolution of the English Farm*, Allen and Unwin, 1952

SMILES, SAMUEL. *The Huguenots*, Murray, 1868

TAYLOR, GLADYS. *Old London Gardens*, Batsford, 1953

THIRSK, JOAN. *English Peasant Farming*, Routledge, 1947

TROW-SMITH, R. *Society and the Land*, Cresset, 1933

YOUNG, ARTHUR. *A Six Month's Tour through the North of England*, Strahan, 2nd Ed, 1771

CHAPTER TWO

CAMDEN, WILLIAM. *Britannia*, 1586

F. N. *The Fruiterer's Secrets*, Printed R.B, 1604. Reprinted as *The Husbandman's Fruitful Orchard*, 1608

GAUT, R. C. *A History of Worcestershire Agriculture and Rural Evolution*, Littlebury, 1939

GERARD, JOHN. *The Herball or General Historie of Plantes*, fol, 1597

GERARD, JOHN. *A Catalogue of Plants Cultivated in the Garden of J. Gerard in the Years 1596-1599*, Ed, B. D. Jackson, 1876

HOGG, ROBERT. *The Fruit Manual*, 5th Ed, Hogg, 1884

HARTLIB, SAMUEL. *His Legacie of Husbandry*, Printed J.M, 1655

LAMBARD, W. *A Perambulation of Kent*, 1596

LETTS, MALCOLM. *As the Foreigner Saw Us*, Methuen, 1935

LISTER, MARTIN. *A Journey to Paris*, 1690

LUCKWILL, L. C. and POLLARD, A. *Perry Pears*, University of Bristol, 1963

MASCALL, LEONARD. *A Booke of the Arts and Maner, Howe to Plant and Graffe all Sorts of Trees etc*, 1572

PARKINSON, JOHN. *Paradisi in sole paradisus terrestris*, 1629

PLAT, SIR HUGH. *The Garden of Eden*, 6th Ed, 1675

SELBY, ELIZABETH. *Teynham Manor and Hundred*, Headley Bros, Ashford, 1936

CHAPTER THREE

BOORDE, ANDREW. *A Compendyous Regyment, or a Dyetary of Helth*, 1542

BRADLEY, RICHARD. *A General Treatise of Husbandry and Gardening*, 1726

CROSSWELLER, W. T. *The Gardeners' Company, 1605-1907*, 1908

GARDENERS' COMPANY. *Scrapbooks*, Guildhall Library, London

FORSTER, JOHN. *England's Happiness Increased*, 1661

GOULD, A. W. *History of the Worshipful Company of Fruiterers of the City of London*, 1912

HAKLUYT, RICHARD. *The Principall Navigations of the English Nations*, 1584

MACHYN, HENRY. *Diary of Henry Machyn 1553-63*, Edited J. G. Nichols, Camden Society, 1848

RILEY, H. T. *Memorials of London and London Life 1276-1419*, 1868

STOW, JOHN. *A Survey of London*, 1598

TIMBS, JOHN. *Romance of London*, 1865

WELCH, CHARLES. *History of the Worshipful Company of Gardeners*, 2nd Ed, 1900

CHAPTER FOUR

BELL, W. G. *The Story of London's Great Fire*, Lane, 1920

DRYDEN, JOHN. *Collected Works*, Edited Saintsbury, 1883

HALL, H. *Society in the Elizabethan Age*, Sonnerschein, 1886

HILL, THOMAS. *The Profitable Art of Gardening*, 1579

PEPYS, SAMUEL. *Diary*. Ed. Wheatley, Bell, 1902

SPENSER, EDMUND. *Collected Works*, Globe Ed, 1899

TUSSER, THOMAS. *A Hundreth Pointes of Good Husbandrie*, 1557

CHAPTER FIVE

ALLAN, MEA. *The Tradescants (1570-1662)*, Michael Joseph, 1964

BRAY, W. *Memoirs of John Evelyn*, Murray, 1871

HADFIELD, MILES. *Pioneers in Gardening*, Routledge, 1935

CHAPTER SIX

CHANCELLOR, E.B. *The Annals of Covent Garden*, Hutchinson, 1920

DANE, CLEMENCE. *London Has a Garden*, Michael Joseph, 1964

JACOB, REGINALD. *Covent Garden*, Marshall, 1913

PASSINGHAM, W. J. *London's Markets*, Sampson Low, 1935

WESTMINSTER LOCAL HISTORY COLLECTIONS. *Newspaper cuttings*, etc. N.D.

CHAPTER SEVEN

FAULKNER, THOMAS. *The History and Antiquities of the Parish of Hammersmith*, Nichols & Sons and others, 1839

LEE, JAMES. *An Introduction to Botany*, Tonson, 1760

LEE, JAMES. *Catalogue of Plants and Seeds sold by Kennedy and Lee*, 1774

WILLSON, E. J. *James Lee and the Vineyard Nursery, Hammersmith*, Hammersmith Local History Group, 1961

WHITTING, PHILIP D. *A History of Hammersmith*, Hammersmith Local History Group, 1965

CHAPTER EIGHT

FORSYTH, W. *Observations on the Diseases, Defects, and Injuries in all Kinds of Fruit and Forest Trees*, London, 1791

FORSYTH, W. *A Treatise on the Culture and Management of Fruit Trees*, London, 1802

HADFIELD, MILES. *Pioneers in Gardening*, Routledge, 1935

SIMMONDS, A. *A Horticultural Who Was Who*, Royal Horticultural Society, 1948

CHAPTER NINE

BAGENAL, N. B. 'T. A. Knight—a sketch'. *The Fruit Year Book 1948*, Royal Horticultural Society

KNIGHT, T. A. *A Treatise on the Culture of the Apple and Pear*, Procter, Ludlow, 1797

KNIGHT, T. A. *A Selection from the Physiological and Horticultural Papers published in the Transactions of the Royal and Horticultural Societies*, Longman, 1841

KNIGHT, T. A. *Pomona Herefordiensis*, London, 1811

SMITH, E. *The Life of Sir Joseph Banks*, Lane, 1911

CHAPTER TEN

FAWKES, F. A. *Horticultural Buildings*, Batsford, 1883

LEMMON, K. *The Covered Garden*, Museum, 1962

SHAW, G. W. *The London Market Gardens*, London, 1879

THOMPSON, J. W. *A Practical Treatise on the Construction of Stoves and other Horticultural Buildings*, 1838

WILKINSON, T. 'Observations on the Form of Hothouses', *Horticultural Transactions*, Vol 1, 1888

CHAPTER ELEVEN

HUNT, JOHN. *Covent Garden Market*, City of Westminster, 1926

LOUDON, J. C. *Encyclopedia of Gardening*, New Edition, Longman, 1860

Southern Railway's Magazine, November/December 1943

CHAPTER TWELVE

MAYHEW, HENRY. *London Labour and London Poor*, Griffin, Vol 1, 1865

SHEARN, W. B. ed. *The Practical Fruiterer and Florist*, Newnes, N. D.

TAYLOR, GEOFFREY. *The Victorian Flower Garden*, Skeffington, 1952

VEITCH, J. H. *Hortus Veitchii*, James Veitch, 1906

CHAPTER THIRTEEN

AQUATIAS, P. *Intensive Culture of Vegetables, French system*, Upcott Gill, 1913

JEBB, L. *The Small-holdings of England*, Murray. 1907

MCKAY, K. D. *The French Garden*, Daily Mail, N.D.

SMITH, THOMAS. *The Profitable Culture of Vegetables*, Longman, 1913

SMITH, THOMAS. *French Gardening*, Joseph Fels and Utopia Press, 1909

WEATHERS, JOHN. *French Market Gardening*, Murray, 1909

CHAPTER FOURTEEN

BURBIDGE, A. W. *Horticulture*, Stamford, 1877

CASTLE, R. LEWIS. *The Book of Market Gardening*, Lane, 1906

EARLEY, WILLIAM. *Profitable Market Gardening*, Upcott Gill, 1882

LUCAS, A. E. Articles in *Middlesex Chronicle*, 1945-7

SHAW, C. S. *The London Market Gardens*, London, 1879

WHITEHEAD, C. *Hints on Vegetable and Fruit Farming*, Murray, 1893

APPENDIX

BUNYARD, E. A. *A Handbook of Hardy Fruits*, Murray, 1920

COATS, A. M. *Garden Shrubs and their Histories*, Vista, 1963

EDLIN, H. L. *British Plants*, Batsford, 1951

GRUBB, N. H. *Cherries*, Crosby Lockwood, 1949

HALL, D. and CRANE, M. B. *The Apple*, Hopkinson, 1933

JOHNSON, A. J. *Garden Names Simplified*, Collingridge, 1931

LOWSON, J. H. *Textbook of Botany*, Revised Howarth and Warne, University Tutorial Press, 1953

NORTHCOTE, R. *The Book of Herbs*, Lane, 1912

OLDHAM, C. H. *Brassica Crops*, Crosby Lockwood, 1942

OLDHAM, C. H. *The Cultivation of Berried Fruits*, Crosby Lockwood, 1948

ROYAL HORTICULTURAL SOCIETY. *Dictionary of Gardening*, Oxford Clarendon Press, 1951

SANDERS, T. W. *Encyclopedia of Gardening*, Revised Hellyer, Collingridge, 1952

SCHWANITZ, F. *The Origin of Cultivated Plants*, Harvard University Press, 1966

SCOTT, J. *The Orchardist*, 1868

STEARN, W. T. 'The Origin and later development of cultivated plants'. *Journal, Royal Horticultural Society*, August, 1965

TAYLOR, H. V. *The Apples of England*, Crosby Lockwood, 1945

TAYLOR, H. V. *The Plums of England*, Crosby Lockwood, 1949

INDEX

Illustrations are indicated by italic figures